M000159044

Gifted Guild's Guide to Depth and Complexity:

Finding Your Way Through the Framework

Gifted Guild's Guide to Depth and Complexity:

Finding Your Way Through the Framework

Ian Byrd

Lisa Van Gemert

Gifted Guild

2019

DEDICATION

for Henry

ACKNOWLEDGEMENTS

The world is a far better place because of the hundreds of thousands of teachers who work tirelessly and selflessly to engage students and enrich their lives. Without you, we would not have set out to write this book in an attempt to help you in some small way. We hope our respect and admiration for you shines through the pages.

To all the educators we've had the wonderful opportunity to meet in professional development, at conferences, through Twitter and in your emails, we want to say thank you for inspiring us and encouraging us in this endeavor. Without your experience and suggestions, this book would not exist.

Had Bette Gould and Sandra Kaplan not created the idea of the framework decades ago, and had Bette's son, John, not carried on the work, Depth and Complexity would not even exist, and so while "thank you" seems insufficient, we offer it. Thank you for sharing the idea of the framework with the world.

To Mary and Steve, our patient spouses, thank you for listening to one side of our phone conversations, brainstorming ideas with us, and supporting us in taking this risk.

Contents

ONBOARD

HAVE YOU HEARD of Depth and Complexity and wondered what it was all about? Have you seen the icons and felt curious about whether that was all there was to it? Have you been using the Depth and Complexity framework, but lack confidence that you're implementing it fully? Have you struggled with taking integration to the next level? Do you ever ask yourself, "But what do you *do* with it?"

If any of these questions sound familiar, you've picked up the right book. In this book, we will introduce you to the framework from scratch, so even if you've never heard of it before, you will be a master by the end. If you are already a power user, we'll be sharing different ways to take your Depth and Complexity practice to the next level.

Why You Need This Guide

Until now, there just hasn't been a comprehensive guide to the Depth and Complexity framework. Learning about it has been a game of telephone. People have relied on one-hour sessions at conferences or the ever-popular Google search. Some lucky individuals have had better training, but it's often a single day, and they're left wondering if they're doing it "right." The results are often less than satisfactory because the people running professional development or writing about Depth and Complexity online have rarely had deep training in the framework. As a result, the same misconceptions and limitations have been passed along like an urban legend. We have longed for a resource that is well-thought out and presented with useful examples for teachers.

That's what this book is for. We have heard the question, "Is there a book?" literally hundreds of times. The answer has always been, "Unfortunately, no." Now, we're happy to say, "Yes, and it's a game-changer."

We're educators who have used the framework in our classrooms with success, and we truly believe in its power to help us raise student thinking. While we're best known in the realm of gifted and talented education, Depth and Complexity is for everyone, and we'll be sharing how it works with all types of learners.

Your Unofficial (Somewhat Irreverent) Guide

This is an unofficial guide, meaning it is not endorsed by, nor connected with, the company that owns the copyright of the icons. Because of that, we may share some ideas that are slightly different from what you've heard before. We are definitely *not* saying that this way is the only way or even the authorized way. One of the issues has been that there *is* no authorized way. That's great for education freedom, but tricky when you're just starting out and want to know how to do something!

We're teachers, so we're sharing ways we have found Depth and Complexity to work best in actual classrooms with real students. Many of the ideas are things we've seen others do and adapted. Unfortunately, we've been doing this a long time and don't remember where we got them all, but just a shout out here to all of the teachers who use Depth and Complexity and have given us great ideas over the years.

Who We Are

We're Ian and Lisa, and we're excited to share our ideas with you. We're writing the book together, and we'll use the term "we" or even sometimes "I" to mean either or both of us, so don't worry about trying to keep track of who is who. Ian is Ian Byrd of byrdseed.com and Lisa is Lisa Van Gemert of giftedguru.com. Together, we founded giftedguild.com, a community for teachers. This new venture is exciting for both of us, and we're particularly excited to be sharing something we both love, Depth and Complexity.

Our hope is that this book will answer all of your questions and, most importantly, get you excited about what Depth and Complexity can do for you in your classroom. We want to take you beyond the pictures to the power that lies in the framework.

Why We Love Depth and Complexity

Do you ever think about all there is to teach your students and feel a little bit like your stomach just fell through your feet? Do you ever look at the gap between where your students are and where they need to be and feel a little dizzy? We truly believe that Depth and Complexity is as close to a one-size-fits-all solution as you can find. It works well with students of diverse backgrounds and abilities, in every content area, and at every grade level.

The book is designed to be practice-based. That means that we'll share the theory and background necessary, and then we'll show you exactly what it looks like in different content areas, a wide variety of grade levels, and with varying student ability dimensions. We'll share real-life work from real-life classrooms. You'll get up close and personal with teachers who are using the framework with great success in their classrooms. You'll get everything you'd get if you were in a face-to-face training with us, and more.

After we introduce you to the framework and what the elements look like in the classroom, we'll share other aspects of implementation. For instance, we'll share how it combines with things you're already using or required to use, like graphic organizers. We'll emphasize combining the framework with Bloom's Taxonomy to raise thinking levels (We use the revised version of Bloom's).

How the Book is Structured

We've structured this book to enable teachers to use it as a guide, hence its name. Part I is an introduction to Depth and Complexity and includes how to introduce the framework to students. Part II explores the elements of Depth and Complexity. The eleven chapters in Part II will explore each of the eleven prompts with these sections:

1. This, not that. In this section we'll explain what this element is and what thinking it tries to elicit. We'll also tell you what it's *not*, which is sometimes even more essential to know. This is where we explain where people go (sometimes horribly) wrong. We'll show good examples and poor ones.

2. How do I introduce it to students? We'll give you at least one way to introduce each element to students so that they are ready to start using them.

3. What are some sample question stems? Avoiding asking only low-level questions or the same questions over and over is tricky. We'll share question stems for each element. Lots of them. It's arguably the most important part of the entire book.

4. What are some sample activities? The moment you've all been waiting for! What does this look like in a real classroom? We'll share ideas for different content areas and grade levels.

Part III examines the five Content Imperatives, Part IV rounds out the rest of the framework, including the idea of disciplinarianism, and the book ends with Part V, which we call "Special Circumstances." In this last section of the book, we explore what the framework looks like in special situations, such as early elementary classrooms, and how it works with graphic organizers, how the elements combine with each other, and how it works with planning.

Like anything else, integrating Depth and Complexity takes practice, and it may not feel natural at first. We promise that over time (and not that much time, either), the framework will become as essential to you as your computer or any other thing you feel you simply cannot teach without. This book is here to guide you to that point. Whether you're a first-year teacher or someone nearing the end of a career, Depth and Complexity will quickly become the lens through which you view your content and the lever you use to lift your students to meet any standard set before you.

Think of this Guide as a resource, not a prescription. We've tried to lay it out in a way that makes sense, yet you are welcome to skip around, using the parts that are of most interest or use to you. You may have seen bits and pieces of what we say here on our websites or in trainings we do. We're bringing it all together under one roof (one cover?), so teachers have a one-stop-shop for all things Depth and Complexity.

Ready? Excited? We are. Let's dive in!

PART I:

AN INTRODUCTION

1

AN INTRODUCTION TO THE FRAMEWORK

WELCOME! WELCOME TO ONE of the most powerful tools in instruction ever created. Our goal in this chapter is to give you a brief introduction to Depth and Complexity and begin to persuade you why it's so wonderful. We'll be going deeper into all aspects of Depth and Complexity throughout the book, so this chapter is our "elevator pitch" combined with some general background.

Because we don't want you to get bogged down with too much information all at once, we're going to introduce you to the Depth and Complexity framework in an FAQ format. Feel free to skip around and read the questions/answers that interest you.

Question: What is Depth and Complexity?

Answer: The Depth and Complexity framework is a set of tools that allow teachers to differentiate for any grade level or content area in a way that is straightforward to implement. It is composed of eleven elements represented by a set of icons or pictures, along with several other components that teachers use to raise the thinking level in the classroom.

The Depth and Complexity framework is primarily a differentiation tool. It adjusts how students approach the content they are learning. The Depth and Complexity prompts are actually part of a longer equation:

differentiation = thinking skill + content + resources + product

Depth and Complexity adjusts content (students will focus on "rules of the gold rush" rather than just the gold rush) but that's not enough. The equation requires us to consider thinking skills (often through Bloom's Taxonomy or Depth of Knowledge). This is perhaps the most common problem in teachers' implementation of Depth and Complexity: they add icons but use them with low-level thinking skills. We will be focusing on pairing Depth and Complexity with high levels of thinking throughout this book.

The equation also asks us to consider what resources students have access to in order to think at a high level (higher-level textbooks, magazine articles, videos, interviews with experts, etc.) and what product students will create to show what they have thought about. When you are differentiating, you can adjust any of those four pieces to meet student needs, interests, and abilities.

In a paper for the California Department of Education published in 1994, these four aspects of advanced learning are outlined: "(1) acceleration/pacing, and planned variations in the (2) depth, (3) complexity, or (4) novelty of curricular tasks" (p. 14). In this paradigm, depth and complexity are fully half of a strong advanced learning program.

Question: How did it begin?

Answer: The Depth and Complexity framework was created by Dr. Sandra Kaplan and Bette Gould for the California Department of Education. It was specifically designed to help teachers in general education classes differentiate for gifted learners.

The Depth and Complexity prompts move students towards expert knowledge of content. Bette Gould and Sandra Kaplan looked to understand how an expert understands their field differently from a layperson. We have heard that they conducted interviews in which they saw that these experts knew things like repeating patterns, required rules, ethical dilemmas, changes over time, and essential vocabulary within their field.

Gould and Kaplan identified eleven of these traits and assigned a name and graphical icon to each. The idea is that students can use these same ways of thinking to move closer to an expert's level of knowledge and understanding. And you can integrate them into your lessons to make sure students are moving toward that expert level.

The contribution of Dr. Kaplan and Bette Gould to the service of gifted children cannot be overstated. The Depth and Complexity model makes differentiation accessible and available to any student in a classroom where a teacher is willing to take a modest amount of time to learn this fantastic model.

Bette's son John, a former teacher himself, offers Depth and Complexity resources for sale (as well as images of the elements for free for personal or classroom use) at the website jtayloreducation.com. We encourage you to visit his site and avail yourself of the resources there.

Question: What's the difference between the framework and the icons?

Answer: The icons represent eleven lenses or tools through which to view and analyze content. Each tool's icon gives students a shortcut to expert thinking. Each image acts as a visual trigger. When your students see an image they recognize, they will know the thinking they should be considering.

The tools' icons especially benefit younger students or those learning English. They unlock access to higher levels of thinking than those students' vocabulary would otherwise support. But their use should not be limited to just those students. Even as a grown man, I (Ian) use the graphical icons when I take notes for my own purposes. If I spot an interesting pattern, I'll draw the patterns icon to call it out. When I see a student draw an icon on their work, I know that they are calling out a certain way of thinking.

A final note about the graphical icons: beware relying on the nice clip art too much. Instead, draw the icons by hand as you teach and encourage students to do the same. The Depth and Complexity prompts are ultimately students' tools and they should be able to use their tools whether or not they have access to the clip art.

The elements of Depth and Complexity are one part of the framework. They are the most common and best recognized, yet they are only one part. We'll be diving into the other components of the framework in this book, so stay tuned!

Questions: What are the elements?

Answer: There are eleven elements, and they are (in no particular order): Across Disciplines, Big Idea, Details, Ethics, Language of the Discipline, Multiple Perspectives, Over Time, Patterns, Rules, Trends, and Unanswered Questions. While each of them is represented by a picture, or icon, the picture is not the element. The element is the thinking lens through which students will analyze content. The eleven elements are what push students to master a subject and understand concepts in a deeper, more complex way.

Question: Why are some elements considered "depth" and some considered "complexity"?

Answer: Of the eleven elements of the Depth and Complexity framework, eight are considered "depth" elements, and three (Change over Time, Multiple Perspectives, and Across Disciplines) are considered "complexity" elements.

In the paper we mentioned earlier that was written for the California Department of Education (Dr. Kaplan was one of the authors), depth "requires students to examine topics by determining the facts, concepts, generalizations, principles, and theories related to them. Depth necessitates uncovering more details and new knowledge related to a topic of study. Depth encourages students to recognize new perspectives. Another way of looking at depth is to mark the difference between a collection of isolated facts and what they become when they are assembled as concepts — the 'big' ideas" (p. 12).

Complexity is explained as "involv[ing] making relationships between and among ideas, connecting other concepts, and layering a why/how interdisciplinary approach that connects and bridges to other disciplines, always enhancing the meanings of ideas" (p. 14).

The elements of the Depth & Complexity framework (also called "prompts") are designed to help teachers help students approach curriculum in these ways.

Question: Can you use the icons and nothing else?

Answer: Can you brush your teeth without toothpaste? Yep. Will it be as pleasant an experience or as effective as with toothpaste? Nope. The elements are more than pictures: they're thinking tools represented by icons. Without the thinking, they're just pictures.

Can you use the elements and not the rest of the framework? Absolutely. It's one of the things we really love about Depth and Complexity; you'll get great results with only one section of it (the eleven elements), but then you can dig deeper and develop your practice. You'll include other aspects of the framework as you become more proficient.

Question: What if you like some of the elements and not others?

Answer: It's a buffet, not a fixed menu, for the most part. Ian wants to vote Trends off the island, while Lisa loves it (see Chapter 9 for that showdown). Most teachers will have go-to elements they default to again and again, and other elements they use rarely, if at all. You will find yourself using some elements more than others, and that's perfectly fine.

You should probably start with trying two or three of the elements and gradually add more as you gain confidence. There is no requirement that you use them all, and there is no order in their implementation. You can begin using any that you wish and add on from there.

Question: How is it better than other strategies?

Answer: We love it because it works with all grade levels and content areas, so no matter what you are teaching, you can use Depth and Complexity. If you move from teaching third grade to teaching high school (it happened to Lisa), you won't have to leave it behind. It will work for you anywhere and always. We've seen it used with kindergarteners through high schoolers.

It also aligns with any standards system. That's important because when your standards change, you can continue using Depth and Complexity. Whether you work with Common Core, state standards, Next Generation Science Standards, or any of the myriad, shifting standards systems, Depth and Complexity will work for you.

We love that it's differentiation made easy. Throughout this book, you'll see examples of differentiation using Depth and Complexity that will shock you in their simplicity. Most teachers' biggest complaint about trying to differentiate is that it takes too much time. With Depth and Complexity, you can differentiate in a matter of seconds or minutes, not hours.

Let's talk about time savings, shall we? Oh, how we love the time a teacher saves when they say, "We're going to look at this through the lens of [insert element of Depth and Complexity] here," and everyone knows what it means. Ah, it makes us happy just thinking about it. Lisa tried to calculate the time savings one year, but gave up at 100 hours. Yep, 100 hours of time saved in planning and instructional time. Who can't use that?

Depth and Complexity rewards educators who are interested in deepening their teaching practice. Because it's such a robust toolbox, you can grow in your understanding and implementation. It never gets old, and there's always room to improve and develop.

Depth and Complexity has been in use since the 1990s. It has survived major changes in education standards and expectations. It is time-tested, so we know that it's not just one more short-sighted idea foisted on teachers.

Question: What can I expect when I start using it?

Answer: You can expect to see results in the form of great discussion and fewer instances of student task confusion ("Wait, what was I supposed to do?") really quickly. You can also expect that, like anything, it'll feel a little awkward and forced at first. Quickly, though, you'll realize that you can't imagine teaching without it.

If other teachers on your campus are using it, it makes it easier because the students have thought alignment (not like George Orwell, though!). You won't have to explain the elements all of the time because your students will have a common vocabulary. Yet even if you're the only teacher on your campus implementing the framework, you'll be surprised at how quickly you will find yourself feeling comfortable with it. Eventually, it will become second nature.

Question: How long will it take my students to understand it?

Answer: Generally, we can get kids up and running with the idea of the framework and a couple of elements in forty-five minutes to an hour. Yep. It's that fast.

We have a whole chapter about introducing the framework to students, so you'll definitely want to explore that in more detail.

Question: Why don't you have the icons in the guide?

Answer: Well, a funny thing happened on the way to the draft of the guide... The images themselves are copyrighted, and that copyright is owned by J Taylor Education. When we began the book, we knew we couldn't use the traditional icons, and at first we felt it was a drawback. However, we quickly realized that we thought was a weakness became a great strength. It's funny how that happens in life.

Ian's wife Mary had the idea to use universal emoji for icons, and this opened up a wonderful world to us. Emoji are much easier to use on devices than the typical icons, the students are familiar with their general look, and they're easy to sketch (We're big, big believers in having students sketch the icons you're using). We didn't put emoji in the guide, but if you want to see our list of the ones we thought were a good fit, visit our page of resources at giftedguild.com/dcextras.

As we were working on the guide, we realized that we didn't need to tell you what to use. Use the icons that work for you. JTaylorEducation generously gives the icons to teachers for free, so use them. Or use emoji. Or use whatever you want. The pictures aren't the point.

The brain is a powerful thing. If I show you a napkin and say, "Every time you see this napkin, I want you to think about lunch time," you will, very quickly, think of lunchtime every time you see a napkin. I can choose any image I want to represent a Depth and Complexity element, and as long as I'm consistent (tree = Big Idea), my students will make that connection. So feel free to substitute. Feel free to sketch. Feel free to adorn your classroom's walls with student interpretations of the icons you choose. If you really want to go all in, let your students crowdsource the icons they want to use to represent the framework's elements.

We use the icons to prompt thinking and to serve as visual cues. They are servants, not masters, so make them work for you.

Wrapping Up

We hope that this brief introduction has answered some of your questions. Neither of us likes education books that go on and on before they finally get to the meat of it, so we've made it brief. You'll learn loads more as you go through the book, and we think all of your questions and concerns will be answered. Just keep in mind: there is no one "right way" – the Depth and Complexity framework looks different in different classrooms, and if you find a way that works for you that is different from what we say, that's fine. We are definitely not the arbiters of Depth and Complexity truth! We're just trying to help you understand and use it in a way that works well for you.

2

Introducing Students to the Framework

WE'RE BIG BELIEVERS in the power of onboarding - getting students interested and engaged before we ask them to jump right into something new. Depth and Complexity is no exception. The time and care we take to introduce it to students will directly affect their interest, acceptance, and ultimately their success in using these tools for them.

Done poorly, Depth and Complexity becomes just one more thing to learn. It's a burden rather than a powerful tool. Done well, student buy-in is smooth, and they will begin using the framework with ease. This is key: students should be using this framework just as much as their teachers, and to make that happen, the framework and elements need to be introduced well. Mary Poppins is right: "Well begun is half done." This is absolutely true of the Depth and Complexity framework. In this chapter, we're sharing how to begin well. We'll explore several ways we've introduced students to the framework. These ideas are neither prescriptive nor comprehensive. There is no "right" way to do it. Hopefully, one of the ideas will work for you, or they will spark an idea of your own that you can use. If you have another idea, we hope you'll share it.

In addition to three ways to introduce the framework as a whole, this chapter explores our thoughts on introducing the individual elements. We're going to share how we introduce each element in the chapter devoted to that element (so you'll see an idea for introducing Details in Chapter 3, an idea for introducing Big Idea in Chapter 4, etc.). In this chapter, we're sharing meta ideas about the introduction of elements in general.

A Framework, Not Just Pictures

One key idea to remember is that you're not introducing pictures: you're introducing a thinking framework. Because of this, we strongly advise against simply taping posters to your wall and calling it good. In fact, even if you're using the official icons, we don't recommend putting up posters until that particular element has been introduced individually. Sorry. We know they're fun and colorful.

Now, if you teach at a school where everyone is using the framework, go ahead and hang up the posters. In this chapter, we're thinking about what you do when your students have never worked with the framework. We're answering the question, "How do you start from scratch?"

As we said, we'll be sharing how to introduce each of the individual elements in the following chapters, but there are some general principles about sharing the framework with students that are important to know.

A note on terminology: We purposefully refrain from calling them "the icons," which degrades these powerful tools to being mere pictures. The names we give things are important! Calling a dinner a "get-together" compared to an "event" will set drastically different expectations. So, rather than "icons," call them "thinking tools" or "prompts" or "elements" of depth and complexity. They truly are tools for deeper and more complex thinking, not just images.

IDEA #1: We're Surrounded by Symbols

This is our favorite strategy, mostly because it's the most comprehensive and works with such a wide range of students. We didn't make it up, but it's the one we use the most. It's also useful if your students may have used the framework in the past and have some familiarity with it because it takes them back to the ideas behind Depth and Complexity. It's the most robust of the ideas, and it takes the longest amount of time (between 25 and 30 minutes, depending upon the group size and age).

To begin, share with students that we are surrounded by symbols. They are all around us. Take a look around the classroom and identify symbols and logos you see (they may be on students' clothing).

The symbols that surround us have different qualities and jobs. They can:

Share information. Symbols share information about what is inside something, what we need to know about something, or where something came from. Amazon boxes have a symbol on them. FedEx trucks have a big logo on the side to tell us packages are inside.

Create an expectation. If I see a Wendy's sign over a building, I have an expectation that I will find fast food (and a frosty!) inside. If I go in and find they're selling tires, I'll be annoyed, even if I need and like tires.

Convey emotion. Emoji tell us a lot about what a person's feeling, don't they? People use them to take the edge off a mean text or instead of writing a whole sentence. A heart shares that we love someone. The symbols can show frustration, concern, anger, joy and pain.

Tell us what to do or not do. If you drive in another country, you can follow the rules even if you don't speak the language because the traffic signs are symbols, rather than words alone. A squiggly arrow tells drivers that the road ahead isn't straight.

Can change meaning over time. Sometimes a symbol that means one thing changes over time to take on a new meaning. Sometimes a symbol can abandon its original meaning completely.

Show the Symbols

Show students a variety of symbols, making sure to include symbols with which they are familiar and that have the characteristics above. Your students' ages will influence the symbols you choose. When you show each symbol, ask them what it means and then discuss it. Here are some examples we use:

- McDonald's: Point out the name (Golden Arches). Why is that better than "Yellow M"? What do you expect when you see a McDonald's sign? Who would be most happy to see one? Least happy?

- Mickey Mouse head silhouette: If you saw this and a McDonald's sign, and you didn't know any more than that, which place would most people rather go? What emotion do most people feel when they see Mickey Mouse ears?

- Nike swoosh: Nike shares this logo with another company. They didn't invent it. It's the symbol of Hermes, the messenger of the gods. He is often depicted with wings on his feet and helmet to symbolize his ability to travel quickly between the world of the gods and the world of humans. Why would Nike want this on their shoes and clothes? What does it imply? The other company that uses this symbol as its logo is FTD florist. Why would a company that delivers flowers want to use this symbol?

- Swastika: This is a symbol that has changed over time. What is it associated with now? This didn't just spring up in the 1930s. It's as old as the Indus Valley Civilization. It's sacred to Buddhists, Hindus, and Jains. It got hijacked by the Nazis. Is it fair for a group to hijack someone's symbol and give it an entirely different meaning?

- Peace symbol: What is this? If you see someone with this on their shirt and they're screaming at their friend in the store, what do you think?

- Poison warning label: This symbol gives us a warning. It tells us not to do something. What happens if you ignore this?

- Shell Oil logo: What is this? What do they sell? Why would a company that sells fossil fuels have a shell as a logo?

- Mercedes-Benz logo: If someone has this on their car, what do we know about the car? If the person driving this car won't donate $1 to the fireman's fund, what do we think?

- Apple logo: Why do you think this has a bite out of it? Is it "b-y-t-e" or "b-i-t-e"? Is it a play on words in the picture?

Note to the teacher: Remember that this list isn't comprehensive. It's illustrative to show how you would discuss the symbols you share. Choose symbols you know your students would recognize. If you are teaching Kindergarten, you may need symbols like Build-a-Bear and other child-friendly icons.

Draw a Symbol

After this discussion, have students work in pairs to come up with a symbol. The constraints are:

- It should be familiar to everyone. No choosing a symbol that only means something to you if you were born in Madagascar 400 years ago. They're not making up a symbol: they're choosing one from the thousands that surround them.

- It should have an emotional response level of at least six on a scale of 1 - 10. This means that it shouldn't just be a "meh" response.

- They should be able to describe its effect or purpose (Create expectation? Convey information? Has it changed over time?)

Have them sketch the symbol on a sticky note and put the sticky notes on a central display space (chart paper or white board, etc.). After every group is done (give just a few minutes), discuss the symbols, categorizing them. Let the pairs explain what they feel their symbol does. Select the one that everyone feels has the strongest emotional response.

If you have students too young to draw out symbols, you may wish to print out a bunch of them and have students choose one to discuss. You can do an internet search for "famous logos" or "well-known symbols."

After this discussion, explain that you will be using a set of eleven symbols in class to help you learn. These symbols are elements of thinking and will do all of the things the symbols we've talked about do; they'll create expectation, convey information, give us a common vocabulary, tell us what to do and not do, and they may adjust meaning from one thing we study to another. They are part of a tool called Depth and Complexity that allows us to use the symbols, and we'll call them "elements" or "prompts." They clue us in to the kind of thinking we're doing. When you see these symbols, these prompts, you will know, "Oh, that prompt is sharing information with me on how I'm supposed to be thinking about this." You will come to know them really well!

The lesson ends here, although you may wish to introduce the first element you wish to share at this time. It's up to you; there is no "right" way. You can download a slidedeck to accompany it at giftedguild.com/dcextras.

Idea #2: A Learning Language

This method is very quick, so it will work well for some teachers. It addresses only one strength of the framework: its commonality of vocabulary. Because of this, it's not as powerful as the idea above. However, if you have a very short amount of time, it's a fine alternative. It also can serve as a refresher of sorts that you can use in the middle of the year to regroup and remind students of one of the purposes of the framework.

To us, the commonality of vocabulary is one of the tremendous strengths of Depth and Complexity. When an entire campus implements the framework, students learn very quickly what a teacher means when he asks the students to use a certain prompt. If everyone is using the same terms, the savings in instructional time is substantial. This is one of the methods we use to share with other educators the power of the framework.

To begin, display a series of words in different languages that all mean the same (e.gl, *ta, danke, merci, gracias*). Ask what the words mean. If someone tells you "thank you" in a language you don't understand, it won't mean that much to you. Ask where you can find definitions for words you don't know and discuss that this takes time to do. It can really interfere with a conversation if you have to constantly pause to look up the meaning of a word.

Explain that the same is true in learning. It speeds things up if we can share ideas without having to explain every word. At this point in the discussion, I (Lisa) like to show a meme of the scene from *A Princess Bride* when Inigo Montoya says to Vizzini, "You keep using that word. I do not think it means what you think it means."

Have them brainstorm a list of subjects from school, being as specific as possible ("division," rather than "math" or "cells" instead of "science" for older students). Choose one. Have students list some of the words we'd need to know in order to talk about studying that subject. For division, we need to know "divisor," "dividend," and "quotient." If we all know those words, our discussion about division is simplified. No one will say, "the thingy on the other side of the thing." Explain that, when we're learning, we also need a set of agreed-upon words that will allow us to think together without constantly explaining what we mean.

To wrap up this introduction, explain that you will be using a set of eleven phrases that will cue students into the type of thinking they'll be doing, no matter what the subject is. They will always know what each word means and will be able to use it whenever they see it.

Idea #3: Introduce Yourself with Frames.

Frames are a commonly used graphic organizer within Depth and Complexity. We devote all of Chapter 24 to them. Even without seeing a frame before, students can get a feel for actually working with the elements of the framework with this activity. One limitation of this particular activity is that it works best at the very beginning of the year, but you have to give them four elements all at once. We've found that they can handle it, though, so don't worry.

First, have students draw a frame (or print one out for very young students). Ahead of time, create a frame about yourself. To do this, put an icon in each section of the frame. I use Details, Rules, Unanswered Questions, and Change over Time.

In each section, write a few things related to that element. Share your frame with your students, emphasizing the elements one by one (Lisa's is below). Explain that in class they will be looking at things they're studying using these elements. Then have them create their own frames, using the same elements you used. I often will have students share with a partner. Then each student will introduce their partner to the class using the frames. I have also done a gallery walk in which students lay their completed frames on their desks. You can display the frames on the classroom walls as well.

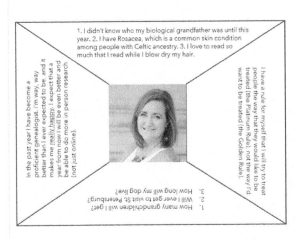

Details: Share three details about yourself that people may find surprising.

Rules: What rules do you follow that you think make you a better friend?

Unanswered Questions: What are three questions about your future that you think you would most like to know the answer to?

Over Time: Pick one of the important ways that you are different now than you were at least one year ago (can be longer). Make one prediction of how you will be different one year from now.

No matter which of these methods you use, Lisa likes to sum up by having students visualize what happens when there's a big evening event happening. The organizers sometimes put those big searchlights out that shoot their beams into the night's sky and draw attention to the location as they spin around. Just like those searchlights, the elements of Depth and Complexity allow us to focus our attention on certain parts of our content. When the light shines on the sky, it highlights one section. The elements of Depth and Complexity do that with our learning.

Thoughts on Introducing Individual Elements

As we said, we'll be sharing how we introduce each individual thinking tool in its own chapter, yet we also wanted to give you some overall tips on introducing the elements to students. If you're introducing the Depth and Complexity thinking tools for the first time to your students, I'd recommend carefully considering your **scope and sequence** for Depth and Complexity.

- Scope: how much am I going to tackle at this time?
- Sequence: what's the best order in which to tackle it?

The school Ian taught at began introducing the prompts of Depth and Complexity in Kindergarten with just a handful (maybe Big Idea, Details, Language, and Unanswered Questions). By second grade all the prompts were in play. Then, teachers of students in upper elementary began combining the prompts or integrating the content imperatives (You'll learn about those in Chapter 14). By the time students went off to middle school, they were ready for even more sophisticated uses.

But not everyone is in a school like this. If you're using Depth and Complexity all by yourself, how do you introduce it all in one year without exploding your kids' brains? The answer is that you don't do it all at once. You will want to start slowly, with one or two at a time. Carefully unroll the elements of the framework like a flower unfurling. Don't shove the whole bouquet in their faces. It's better to have students familiar with a few than confused about many. The grade level you teach will influence the speed with which you introduce the elements, as will the level of school-wide implementation.

We think it's important to introduce new elements of Depth and Complexity using content your students are familiar with. Begin by analyzing a popular movie, restaurant, game, or person before integrating a prompt with grade-level content. In other words, always practice new prompts with well-known content.

Pair Them Up

Ian likes the following sequence because it groups prompts that add to each other. Spend a week or so on each group so that students get a chance to really practice. No sense in rushing.

1. **Big Idea and Details:** I introduce these first since they're the easiest to grasp and are clearly opposite. Because they're opposites, they work well as a pair. Details will reveal Big Ideas. Big Ideas need Details as support.

2. **Rules and Patterns:** These often seem similar, so introducing them together allows you to highlight their differences. Rules represent things that *must* be followed or there's a negative consequence (hierarchies, laws, social norms) and Patterns represent things that often repeat, but don't *have* to repeat. Think of it this way: when Rules break, there's a problem. When Patterns break, it's interesting.

3. **Ethics, Multiple Perspectives, and Over Time:** I think Ethics and Multiple Perspectives go hand-in-hand. How do *different folks* see the same problem? But we can also

use Change over Time to supplement Ethics. How has a problem *changed?* I'd also emphasize that we can combine each of these prompts with each of the other prompts we've learned as well. Ethics and Rules are beautiful together.

4. **Language of the Discipline and Across the Disciplines:** I've found that the word "discipline" is easily misinterpreted. Kids (and their parents!) can think we mean "punishment" rather than "area of study." These can go together to emphasize that each discipline has its own tools, but we can also go across disciplines and bring those tools with us.

5. **Unanswered Questions** was my most under-utilized prompt, so I might introduce it all by itself to give it the spotlight. Along with Big Idea (often confused with simply a topic), Unanswered Questions is the other mis-used element. It's not just what students want to know – it's much deeper than that – so it's nice to introduce it all by itself. What are the things that are *unknowable?*

Ian thinks you should just throw Trends in wherever you want (or just vote it off the island), but Lisa doesn't, so get ready for her strenuous defense of Trends in Chapter 9.

Organic Introduction

Lisa has a different method for introducing the elements. Neither is right or wrong: it's just what we do. You may choose one of these orders, or you may branch out and do one entirely of your own making or choosing. There is no required order.

Lisa begins with Details and Rules because she uses the Rules element in her classroom management strategy (see more about that in Chapter 6). She uses Details to introduce the students to each other in the beginning of the year. So, both of those elements come first because they are what fit her content.

She decides which element(s) to introduce next based on what she's teaching. For instance, if the topic is plot or the water cycle (or anything "cycle"!), you're going to need Patterns, so introduce Patterns next. If you're exploring something with important vocabulary, then Language of the Discipline is the element of choice. If you're teaching a historical event, it may be a good opportunity for Multiple Perspectives.

Lisa slowly adds in more elements as they naturally fit her content. Usually, she introduces one or two elements a week until the students have all of them in their toolbox. It may be three months into the school year before all eleven are in play, and that's fine.

It's not just the content that leads towards a specific element: it's also the thinking. The Ethics element is what we use for pro/con discussions, so we'd need to introduce that before any of those discussions take place. As you read through the chapters for each element of Depth and Complexity, consider how your content matches up. As you grow in understanding of the prompts of Depth and Complexity, you'll find that it becomes second nature to gravitate towards one prompt or group of prompts for any given topic or activity.

Wrapping Up

Remember that these ideas are not the only options. They may spark an idea of your own, or you may wish to stick closely to these. You may choose to try a couple of different ways, or even combine them. Ideas #1 and #3 go well together, with Idea #1 being used first. If one doesn't work for you, try a different one. Whatever way you choose to introduce the framework, the most important thing is to convey your own confidence and excitement about Depth and Complexity. You'll find that students will often return to you the same attitude you send to them.

PART II:

THE ELEMENTS OF DEPTH

AND COMPLEXITY

3

DETAILS

THE DETAILS PROMPT ASKS, "What makes this thing different, unique, and special? In what way is this distinguished from other, similar things? Why are those differences important? Which of those Details is worth considering? Which of them are not?"

Details: What It Must Do

Details make your students get specific. Like a detective with a magnifying glass, students use Details to zoom in. They inspect, compare, and evaluate evidence that must eventually lead to a larger idea. A detective who gathers every clue at the crime scene and then packs up for the day has obviously not finished their job. The clues themselves are material to build a case. Students' use of Details *must not* stop at "making a list." They must ponder those Details and move towards Patterns, Rules, Big Ideas, or other more-abstract prompts of Depth and Complexity. Details must lead students to do something.

Details: This, Not That

Do you think Details are just facts? Do you get all list-y with Details? Do you think of it is as really low level, like the basement of Bloom's? If so, you are doing Details a big disservice.

The most common problem with how folks use Details is to pair it with the lowest-level thinking skills and then stop and move onto another question. Students can certainly make lists of Details, but they must move on to analyze or evaluate those lists.

> Instead of This: "List at least ten Details about Abraham Lincoln."
>
> Try This: "Which of those Details about Abraham Lincoln do you feel are most important in relation to the Civil War? How can you support that opinion with evidence from the text?"
>
> Or This: "Compare those Details to your list of George Washington. What Patterns do you notice between these two presidents?
>
> Or This: "Looking at your list, how can you summarize Abraham Lincoln in one sentence?"

You don't need Depth and Complexity for students to make a list. Used correctly, Depth and Complexity must push students' thinking.

The second problem we see is allowing students to settle for any ol' Details. The detective with the magnifying glass is constantly evaluating the importance of their clues. Students must know that all Details are not created equal. Do not accept details that are obvious, trivial, or irrelevant.

When introducing this to students, we emphasize *essential* Details. The number of hairs in Abe Lincoln's beard is certainly a specific detail, but it's pretty inessential. His major accomplishments, his past as a lawyer, and each of his failures to be elected would be essential details. In a story, essential details would include the main characters, major plot events, the time period and so on. Obviously inessential details might include the number of commas in the story. That may seem like an oversimplification, but many students (and teachers, if we're honest with ourselves) sometimes focus too long and too hard on the inessential details.

This: Why does the author need us to understand the physical appearance of the character?
Not This: What does the character look like?

This: Which factors in the rise of the Roman Empire made it most vulnerable to later collapse?
Not This: What are the factors in the growth of the Roman Empire?

This: Which latitude is most likely to have a greater amount of sunlight during its winter, this or this?
Not This: Latitude is expressed in degrees and minutes.

This: Which of the techniques we've learned is most essential to solving the problem correctly?

Not This: What techniques have we learned?

It's important for students to know that when we're looking at Details, we're looking at the essential and distinguishing characteristics and attributes of something, but

It's equally important for students to know that they have to actually analyze those Details – comparing, contrasting, evaluating, and connecting – not just recognize and identify.

Details may be seen or unseen, so they're not just descriptions. The Details prompt enables math students to identify the important words in a story problem, science students to ignore superfluous data, social studies students to focus on factors that led to conflict or resolution, and language arts students to hone in on what attributes of a character contributed to the conflict in the story.

Another issue we see with Details is teachers not using Details to lead into and support other elements. For example, it's poor scholarship (and annoying) when someone shares a Big Idea with no support for it. Details is often the element that solves that problem. Details support Big Ideas. Details are what make up Patterns. Details are what usually Change over Time. Details are what we notice Across Disciplines. Details are what inform Trends. If there were an Academy Award for the elements of Depth and Complexity, Details would walk away with Best Supporting Actor hands down, with a mic drop.

So, make sure that you are leveraging the power of Details to support the broader arguments students are making with other elements.

This: Because of these factors, we can understand this Big Idea.

Not This: Here's my great big unsupported Big Idea.

This: These Details combine to create this Pattern.

Not: Here's this Pattern that sprang out of nowhere.

Recognizing the role that Details plays as a supporter of other elements is not an invitation to keep it low-level. Analyzing the Details is what makes the eventual conclusion powerful, effective, and valid.

What are Some Sample Question Stems?

Low Level Questions (Beware!)

- List the details of _____.
- What are the details of _____?

Analyze

- Compare the attributes of _____ with _____. Include [give constraints here].
- Which details are true of both _____ and _____?
- In what important ways does this differ from _____?
- How does [this part] impact or affect [this part]?

- Which Details appear in both this Pattern and that Pattern? Do they perform the same function in both Patterns?

Evaluate

- Which features are the most important characteristics of _____?
- In this problem, which details are irrelevant?
- Of the ideas we associate with _____, which are the least likely to endure?
- Which details are missing from this analysis/graph/summary?
- Does this detail prove or disprove the Big Idea _____?
- What Details apply most accurately/logically/importantly to ___?
- Which Details best support the Big Idea that ___?

Synthesize

- How would you determine if this characteristic were essential?
- Which details would [insert character] be most likely to leave out when he/she retold the story in order to make him/herself look better than he/she really is?
- What would happen if we eliminated _____? Would it change in an important way?
- What do the details suggest/reveal about ___?

What are Some Sample Uses?

Because the key to using Depth and Complexity is adjusting students' thinking upwards, all classroom uses should focus on questioning and thinking, not a printable worksheet.

Details can be very straightforward. This is Details task: The tens' column is _____ times the value of the ones' column and _____ the value of the hundreds' column.

And so is this: In the number 5,496, which number is in the column that is one-tenth the value of the column that has the 4 in it?

Details questions should also require some analysis, as we explained above. Consider the novel *Charlotte's Web*. These are Details questions related to that novel: How was Fern a friend to Wilbur? How was Templeton a friend to Wilbur? Who was the most important friend to Wilbur?

If you're a Thinking Maps® user, Details is a perfect fit with a Bubble Map® or Double Bubble® map. You would also use Details with a Flow Map® because a sequence is composed of Details.

Have you used sociograms before? Sociograms originated as a way to show how characters in a story are connected with one another, but they can be used in any content area to show details. (See an example at giftedguild.com/dcextras.)

Instead of having students highlight important ideas or pieces of information, have them sketch a quick Details icon next to them.

Have students identify the most important details and then defend their choices to a partner.

Give students a Big Idea, and then let students support that with proof.

How Do I Introduce It to Students?

As mentioned, you can introduce Details with a simple discussion comparing essential and non-essential details about something. If you do this, it's nice to start with something students know a lot about, even if it's not what you're teaching. That way, they have something to contribute to the discussion.

You can also use the Details element to introduce the students to each other or introduce them to the classroom. Lisa does an exercise where she has students start listing details about themselves on paper. While they're thinking of things, she walks around throwing out ideas until she sees that most students have a number of things written down. She prompts students with suggestions such as:

- How many brothers and sisters do you have?
- If someone gave you a gift card to a store, which store would you want a gift card from?
- What's your favorite thing to have for dinner?
- Have you ever broken a bone?
- Do you have a pet? If so, what is it?
- Do you wish you had a pet?
- What's your favorite flavor of ice cream?

- Where would you like to go on vacation?
- If you could only listen to one song the rest of your life, what would it be?
- Do you have a favorite stuffed animal? (Yes, even her high school students have them!)
- What's your favorite color?
- What's your favorite season?
- What's your favorite time of day?
- When you were really little, what book did you want to read over and over?
- Would you rather be too hot or too cold?
- What's a favorite piece of clothing you have?
- If you didn't have the name you have, what's a name you would like to be called?

Once the students all have at least five or so, she has them pair up with a shoulder partner. The shoulder partners share their details, and then they introduce each other to the rest of the class using a few of the details (not all). To do this, they say, "This is my friend, So-and-So. So-and-So has three dogs and wants a guinea pig. He loves any flavor of ice cream except ones with nuts. He loves his blue hoodie so much that he wears it no matter how hot it is."

While they are doing this, Lisa actively makes connections from student to student. She'll say, "Oh! You have a dog! Who else has a dog?" In this way, students build community early on. It's surprising how many students who have gone to school together for years don't know some fundamental details about each other.

After this, it's a good exercise to pick a common item like a house and have students analyze it through the lens of Details. What are its unique characteristics and features? What makes it different from other similar items? Which of these characteristics is/are irrelevant? Which are crucial? Which are common? Which are rare?

4

Big Idea

THE BIG IDEA IS NOT THE TOPIC. It's what we can *say about* the topic having learned about it. Big Idea has the honor of being one of the most misunderstood/misused elements, while simultaneously being one of the most important for developing critical thinking in students. Big Idea is the element that allows students to analyze information and then answer, "So what?" when asked to crystalize their analysis.

Big Idea: What It Must Do

The Big Idea tool must make your students think abstractly. It must get them to zoom out and see the content from a 10,000 foot view. Just like when you fly in a plane, small details become irrelevant, but larger ideas suddenly become visible. You can see things from a plane that you could not from the ground. Likewise, Big Idea must make your students see content in a new way.

Big Idea: This, Not That

Big Ideas that do not achieve their purpose fall into a couple of categories:

Merely re-stating the topic (we see this *all the time*):

- George Washington
- polygons
- *Where the Red Fern Grows*

Trivial statements about the topic:

- George Washington was a president.
- A square is a shape.
- *Where the Red Fern Grows* is about a boy and his dogs.

You don't need Depth and Complexity for students to write down those ideas! They're obvious. Big Idea *must* make your students see content in a new way or you're not really using it.

Instead of these poor examples, students should produce complete sentences (yes, we need to say this) that require evidence and could possibly be argued against. Big Ideas should be *interesting* and show that students have benefited from purposefully switching to a 10,000 foot view.

Better Big Ideas:

- George Washington was a president who faced difficult decisions (a solid Big Idea for younger students)

- George Washington made the best choices he could at the time
- A square is the most perfect of shapes
- *Where the Red Fern Grows* shows that loss makes us grow (spoiler!)

Let's put them side by side to show the difference:

A Big Idea: An unbalanced equation has not truly been solved.

A Topic: balanced and unbalanced equations

A Big Idea: The number zero is the most powerful number.

A Topic: multiplying by zero

A Big Idea: The democratic system of government allows for tremendous freedom, yet requires tremendous diligence on the part of citizens.

A Topic: democracy and freedom

These Big Ideas show that students *thought.* They looked from up high at all the information before them and pulled out a larger, abstract idea that would be invisible from the ground. It's key to note that a Big Idea builds on the other prompts of Depth and Complexity. You cannot arrive at a Big Idea without considering Details, Patterns, Ethics, and so on. Asking students to consider Big Idea first, without including an analysis of these more specific prompts, can lead to weak, unsupported Big Ideas. Depth and Complexity exists as a system, not isolated ideas.

Let Big Idea Be Purpose Driven

Big Idea might also prompt students to think about the *purpose* of a topic. Why do we even need to put numbers into sets? What's the Big Idea of a school or a family? Also, ask what would happen if we *didn't* have or do that thing? For example, a Big Idea of animal classification could be, "Organizing animals in descending, smaller groups makes it easier to identify new species and sub-species." Have students challenge that idea with questions like, "What would happen if we didn't organize animals in the animal kingdom? How would it really impact us?"

A Big Idea might be a motto or a saying, such as "A stitch in time saves nine." Have students examine that. Is it true? When is it not? Where did the idea come from? When applied to a person, the Big Idea might sum up their life's accomplishments, their personality, or their purpose. What's the Big Idea of Martin Luther King? How about Luke Skywalker? Cleopatra? What is their "so what"?

The Big Idea of *Where the Red Fern Grows* could be as simple as a summary of the plot, but it could also be the story's theme or moral, or the author's purpose. In language arts classes, teachers will use Big Idea to explore theme in fiction and main idea in non-fiction.

Big Ideas can (and often *should*) go beyond one topic. For example, the big idea "Growing up requires sacrifice" can be found in many stories, films, and in historical contexts. Because of this, we can use the Big Idea to connect within and across disciplines.

Should the Teacher Provide the Big Idea or Should Students Generate Big Ideas?

You should do both! Understand that each option leads to a dramatically different way of thinking and choose your path purposefully.

If you ask students to look at a bunch of information and form a Big Idea, they are using Inductive Thinking (or parts-to-whole thinking). Kids don't typically get a lot of practice thinking inductively at school. It can be messy since students can end up with ideas you may not have predicted. But it reflects real-world thinking. Rarely are we given a Big Idea in the beginning of the day to guide us. We have to make decisions all the time based on the Details around us. And boy does Inductive Thinking give the brain a workout. It moves students right up Bloom's Taxonomy. Like a detective, they're analyzing clues and then synthesizing to create a summary of all that information. There's intellectual excitement when a student gathers a bunch of clues and arrives at the Big Idea, "It was the Butler!"

When you give students a Big Idea and ask them to prove or disprove it, they are thinking Deductively (Note that Sherlock Holmes mixes these two terms up! What he calls "deduction" is actually "induction!" Kids love this fact.). While inductive thinking has the advantage in terms of forcing students to deal with the messy process of creating a Big Idea, deduction has its own advantages. Most notably, when the teacher creates the Big Idea, you can *push* students further than they'd go on their own. You can generate a Big Idea that is a bit beyond your students' typical reach. You can offer them something unexpected. When the teacher offers students a Big Idea to consider, it *must* be a Big Idea that the class wouldn't have come up with. Then you can get them thinking in a different way than if they created their own Big Idea.

For example: if you're reading The Three Little Pigs, don't give kids the Big Idea "Hard work pays off." Come on. That won't push even the youngest of kids. It's too obvious. Instead, your Big Idea should force their thinking in a new direction. Try one of these:

- "Sometimes it's better to plan ahead and sometimes it's better to make it up as you go."
- "Power can be seen or unseen" (you'll see this one again in our section about Universal Themes).
- "Failing to plan is planning to fail."
- "The enemy of my enemy is my friend. Even if it's my brother I'm mad at."
- "Not all fortresses are equally powerful."

As always, the focus should be on what students are doing with their brains.

Combine It with Details

We like to share Big Idea and Details together because they help define each other. The Big Idea is all about a summary, generalization, or opinion of an idea, while Details highlights the essential characteristics.

Any time we form a Big Idea, we need details to back it up. If I state that George Washington was the greatest of presidents (that's a nice Big Idea), I had better have some specific details to prove my point. If I call Disneyland "the happiest place on earth," I need some evidence, or details, to show that it's true (or at least possible). Big Idea and Details go together like peanut butter and jelly.

The Big Idea allows students to say, "Because I know all of this, I can say..." Students shouldn't just identify the Big Idea, but also explain it, compare or contrast it with the Big Idea of related content, and argue for their Big Idea. Simply identifying a Big Idea without supporting the reasoning behind it results in opinion alone, rather than analysis. That's not what we're going for with students.

Interestingly, the Big Idea of very complex things may be simple, and the reverse is also true. Sometimes, a student will be able to distill a very simple, elegant Big Idea from a set of complex data points. Other times, students will examine simple things and come up with very complex Big Ideas. Both of these scenarios are fine.

Big Idea is what we will frequently use in science and social studies classes when we explore principles, laws, or theories. At the end of an experiment, the Big Idea will bring our results to explanatory fruition. In Lisa's high school political science classes,

Big Idea plays a huge role. How does the Big Idea of the theory of socialism fare when challenged by its actual implementation?

If a math teacher can get students to pull out a quality Big Idea from the lesson, it serves as a check for understanding. What is the Big Idea of this lesson/chapter/unit? What is the most important thing to know?

It looks different in a third grade class, of course, but the idea is the same. How does the Big Idea of the water cycle differ from the Big Idea of the life cycle of the plant? Sometimes grade level is unimportant. Some Big Idea analysis self-differentiates across grade levels. Consider which grade this would be appropriate for: "In what way does the Big Idea of this story differ from the Big Idea of the story we read just before this?" If you said, "almost any grade," you'd be right, and that, friends, is one of the great powers of Depth and Complexity.

What Are Some Sample Question Stems?

Low Level Thinking (Beware!)

- What is the Big Idea of _____?

Analyze

- How does the Big Idea of _____ compare to the Big Idea of _____?
- Which Details argue against this Big Idea?
- What else can we apply this Big Idea to that we've learned previously?

- If this Big Idea is true for _____, what else might it be true for?

- In what ways is the Big Idea of this different from a Big Idea about this topic you've seen before?

Evaluate

- Using at least three elements of the Depth & Complexity framework, support the Big Idea that _____.

- Which of these statements best supports the Big Idea that _____? In order to agree with this Big Idea, what ideas or facts do we need to accept? Does this Big Idea have a winner or a loser?

- How does the value of the idea taught in this lesson compare the to the value of the idea taught in yesterday's lesson? Which one is more useful? Defend this opposing Big Idea. How could you begin to try to prove this Big Idea is not valid?

- What information would change your mind about this Big Idea?

Synthesize

- What overarching statement can we make to best define/describe _____?

- Who or what is most likely to object to/agree with this Big Idea?

- How important is this Big Idea? What makes it more or less important? To whom would it/could it be the most important?

What Are Some Sample Uses?

Big Idea can be used either deductively or inductively. To use it deductively, the teacher would give the students the Big Idea (e.g., Competition for natural resources leads to conflict) and have them come up with Details to support that. To use it inductively, students would examine a number of Details and infer a Big Idea from them. You either move from Details to Big Idea (inductive) or Big Idea to Detail (deductive).

You could ask students to identify the Big Idea of:

- A document like the US Constitution
- A concept like the periodic table of elements or plate tectonics
- A story, poem, or play
- A math topic like division
- A character or historical figure

Students' answers will vary depending on their own sophistication. One student might see the Big Idea of the Constitution as "the rules of the United States," but another might say that it's "a tool to protect citizens from their leaders." Both can be correct if justified with evidence (and the evidence is represented by the Details prompt).

While students should generate their own Big Ideas, you might also offer your own for them to consider. Your Big Ideas should challenge their thinking, forcing new connections. And it's always possible to disagree with someone's Big Idea, even if that person is the teacher!

As with the other elements of Depth & Complexity, Big Idea looks different in different content areas, yet works in all of them. If you're discussing a story, the Big Idea might be:

- The theme or author's message
- A summary
- An opinion about the story

For science, the Big Idea might be:

- The result of the experiment or series of experiments
- A summary of a series of related laws
- A commentary on the reproducibility or validity of an experiment

For math, the Big Idea might be:

- An encapsulation of what is possible with a set of numbers or laws/corollaries
- A description of patterns seen
- A position on the usefulness or application of a theorem or strategy

In social studies, the Big Idea might be:

- A synopsis of a historical figure's contribution

- A description of the impact of an event
- Defining the value of a geographic influence
- An overarching look at a particular location's current or past relevance/environmental health, etc.

In art/music, the Big Idea might be:

- A statement about the aesthetic quality of a particular work or material
- A summary of an artistic movement

In physical education, the Big Idea may examine:

- The goal of the rules of a game
- The overall impression of an athlete
- The result of practice or effort

We've just given a few examples here from different content levels, yet we think they're enough for you to see the pattern emerge: Big Idea is about the Big Picture.

Scaffold Students into More Powerful Big Ideas

Caution: if you let them, students will give you low-quality Big Ideas. Sometimes this is intellectual laziness, but sometimes it's simply that they didn't see the possibilities. They need help in crafting strong Big Ideas. This isn't just true of young students. Even high school students (ahem, even *adults*) often struggle to get in the habit of identifying strong Big Ideas. Want proof? Just ask any adult you know what they think the Big Idea of government or the Big Idea of dinner is. Often, you will get pat, clichéd responses, or pithy quotes they've heard ("Oh, it's of the people, by the people, for the people."). We're not being judgmental of students when we say this: Humans in general will offer shallow thinking unless guided to deeper intellectual waters.

In order to support students in their pursuit of a valid Big Idea, we often recommend scaffolding their thinking. There are three approaches to this. First, you can make sure they have the opportunity to explore the content thoroughly before asking them to generate a Big Idea. Shallow experience = shallow Big Idea. Make sure you check for understanding before you unleash them on a Big Idea to make sure they have the mastery they need.

You can also share a Big Idea with them and use it as a touchstone throughout the content ("How do you think this ties in with our Big Idea of _____?"). Keep returning to it over and over, evaluating how new information or ideas aligns with it. Revise it if necessary. Starting with one Big Idea, and then revising it through a unit, is a powerful technique.

A third way to support students in developing Big Ideas is to give them a Big Idea template. They fill in certain words, but the structure is provided. This works very well with younger learners in particular, but even high school students can benefit from it. Here are some ideas for scaffolds:

- If _____ had not happened, _____ would have been changed in that_____.

- We are _____ for _____. (e.g., responsible/behavior; only on Earth/short time; built/relationships)
- Struggle leads to _____.
- If I _____ then I should expect _____.
- Sometimes what _____ isn't _____.
- In the end, what really _____ is _____.

You can even provide a word bank of choices if you want to support younger or struggling students. The Big Idea of a scaffold is that students will develop a feel for what makes a solid Big Idea when they have support in developing them.

How Do I Introduce It to Students?

Sometimes Ian introduces it by saying "imagine you're trying to explain an idea to an alien in one sentence." This is a quick and effective way to get students to understand that with Big Idea, we're trying to capture the essence of something.

Author Dan Pink gave Lisa the idea she uses to introduce Big Idea. It takes a little longer, but it's one of her favorite things all year. It's called "What's Your Sentence?" In Pink's book, *Drive: The Surprising Truth about What Motivates Us*, he shares the idea that everyone has (or should have) a sentence that encapsulates what their life is about. You can have students create their own sentence and let that lead to the idea that Big Idea is the "What's Your Sentence?" of the content we're analyzing.

Students love this and it's very simple to do. You can get the specifics and a printable to use with your students at giftedguru.com/whats-your-sentence.

A third way to introduce Big Idea is to tell a fable, such as the tortoise and the hare. Ask students to think of a Big Idea of the fable. All of Aesop's fables have Big Ideas that are easy to detect, such as "slow and steady wins the race." Tell a couple of more (they're all short), asking each time, "What's the Big Idea?" Explain to students that the Big Idea prompt asks them to take what they have learned and capture it all in a single sentence.

5

LANGUAGE OF THE DISCIPLINE

LANGUAGE OF THE DISCIPLINE EXPLORES the vocabulary and tools used in a given field. The average third grader has a vocabulary of about 10,000 words, and the average twelfth grader has 40,000. The acquisition of those 30,000 words is dependent to a great extent upon the vocabulary learned in school. Many of us are well aware of how problematic it is when students don't know or misunderstand key academic vocabulary. That's the job of Language of the Discipline.

Language of the Discipline: What It Must Do

Language of the Discipline gives students the tools to communicate effectively. Imagine visiting a doctor who calls your neck your "head connector thing" or your femur the "top leg bone." Those labels are not *wrong,* yet you'd probably seek a second opinion. Knowing a discipline's proper language is essential to being able to communicate about it. When someone gets the language wrong, they seem like absolute beginners. When using Language of the Discipline, it must move students towards communicating like experts of the field.

Language of the Discipline: This, Not That

The most common problem we see with this prompt is just plopping an icon next to an existing list of vocabulary or spelling words. Depth and Complexity must change our students' thinking. Language of the Discipline is not spelling words: it's the academic vocabulary that experts would use.

Don't be satisfied with the list of vocabulary words provided before a lesson, really consider how an expert would discuss the topic.

This means thinking about:

- the tools of a discipline ("Bunsen burner" or "protractor" or "easel")
- signs or symbols (common in math and science, but also consider a compass rose in social studies)
- idiomatic expressions or jargon
- the people of a field (Pythagoras is language of the mathematical discipline)
- acronyms and other mnemonic devices ("FANBOYS" for coordinating conjunctions)
- how words may be used differently across content areas ("expression" does not mean the same thing in math that it does in language arts)

Depth and Complexity must push our practice and our students' thinking forward, not just re-label an existing list.

It's Important, and It's More Than Just Vocabulary

We're big believers in the power of mastering academic vocabulary. One year when Lisa was teaching high school English, a large number of students in her state (Texas) failed the sophomore level state assessment because they didn't understand one of the words in the essay prompt. Even though they were allowed to use dictionaries and thesauruses, they didn't (shocker). They responded inappropriately and skewed the scores significantly.

If a discipline has specific skills or tasks, those fall under this element, as well. Consider the skills of diagramming sentences, crafting a thesis statement, sketching a topographical map, recognizing a map projection, plotting coordinates on a graph, and all of the other myriad skills unique to specialized content areas. All of these are Language of the Discipline.

Additionally, any idiomatic expressions or jargon used in the domain is also part of this element. These can be the most challenging for language learners, and Depth and Complexity can be very helpful in adding a visual overlay to tricky text.

Famous figures or people are part of this. So, Pythagoras is Language of the Discipline! Frequently, content standards in social studies require knowing certain historical figures, and these can be approached through this lens. When you think of it that way – as key vocabulary – it opens up a world of possibilities for activities.

Lastly, acronyms used in the field fit in this element as well. "PEDMAS" for the Order of Operations, "FANBOYS" for coordinating conjunctions, in addition to other pneumonic devices all fall under Language of the Discipline. As you can see, it's more than just spelling words!

One of the reasons it's so critical for students to truly master academic vocabulary (in addition to the apparent and bizarre reluctance to look up words in, you know, a dictionary), is that the same word can have different meanings in different content areas. For example, "conflict" means something different in social studies than it does in language arts. This nuance is part of what makes Language of the Discipline such a useful element.

It's Needed More than You May Realize

Many folks just see this too narrowly. They think that if a discipline doesn't have official lists of terminology, that there isn't a Language of the Discipline. Sometimes when we're working in a content area for long time, we get so used to its lexicon that we don't realize there is one (This is called the Curse of Knowledge. Look it up! -Ian).

To avoid this error, consider thinking about the words that your students frequently misuse. Do you ever notice when a student uses a word incorrectly in a way that can (or could) cause confusion? That's a great place to start. Next, look at your standards. Scan them to see words that are not used in all content areas.

Just to test this idea, we pulled up the CCSS 7th Grade math standards. The first introductory paragraph contained no fewer than eleven words or phrases that were Language of the Discipline candidates (proportional relationships, operations, rational numbers, expressions [which has a very different meaning from language arts], linear equations, scale drawings, geometric constructions, area, surface area, volume, and populations). Language of the Disciplines is *everywhere.*

How Do I Introduce It to Students?

Ian learned to introduce the elements using a hamburger or bicycle and these are perfect for pointing out how important it is to know the language of *any* discipline, even the cooking of a burger!

I'd point to the bun (without saying the word) and ask students if we should call this "the bread." Well, it's *really* called "the bun." I'd goof around and ask why it matters. It is bread, *is it not*? This leads us into a discussion about specifics. See, "bun" is a specific type of "bread." A hamburger made with two slices of toast would be... *weird.* It matters to be specific and use the proper language of the discipline. I'd do the same thing with the patty, asking if we should just call it "the meat" or "the beef." It's not that it's wrong, but it just isn't right *enough.* You would be surprised if a hamburger arrived with a pile of ground beef rather than a beef patty, right?

This works with all kinds of student-friendly topics. In baseball, we don't call home plate a "base." It's a "plate." There are not "points," there are "runs." If someone makes these language mistakes, it's obvious that they are new to baseball. You could have students consider their own hobbies and think about the specific language they use.

Lisa has a script of her introduction. Of course, this is just one idea, and you are free to come up with a different idea or to modify this one to meet your needs/grade level.

Sample Script to Introduce Language of the Discipline:

Just think of the answer to this in your mind: Which of these words would you expect to hear from a doctor, "prescription" or "swimming pool?"

Which of these words would you expect to hear at the grocery store, "milk" or "car"?

These were simple questions, weren't they? They were simple because we are familiar with what words go with what places and people and professions.

If you went to a doctor for a broken arm and she said, "Oh, that bone in your arm is broken. I don't remember what that bone is called, but I know exactly how to fix it," would you believe her?

If you meet a new friend who says he plays soccer but can't name the position he plays, would you think he played very much?

Think for seven seconds about why it is important to know the words for things if you want to be taken seriously.

[After seven seconds, call on students for responses.]

Words that are specific to a job or a sport or a class in school are called Language of the Discipline. Sometimes in textbooks, you'll find these words and their definitions in the back in what is called the "glossary." Sometimes, they will be in bold.

[If your textbook has a glossary, pull it out and explore a few of the words you find there. If not, move forward. Divide students into groups of three or five. Have a student in each group sketch out a Venn Diagram labeled "Regular Words" and "Language of the Discipline."]

As a group, complete the diagram with characteristics of the two types of words, and where the circles overlap, share characteristics of both types of words. You have five minutes to come up with as many ideas as possible.

[You may wish to do this as a whole class exercise. If the students complete it themselves, after five minutes, bring the class back together. Sketch your own Venn Diagram. Ask each group for one idea from each of the three spaces, filling out the diagram as you go. It's best to ask this in a random pattern, one circle at a time, rather than having one group list their three words in a row. Discuss where the responses are similar and where they are different.]

One of the reasons Language of the Discipline is important is to save time. If a doctor had to say, "I'm going to give you a piece of paper for you to take the pharmacy so they know what medicine to give you and how much of that medicine you need and how often you should take it," it would take a lot more time than saying, "I'm going to give you a prescription."

In order to talk about [insert the name of your content or grade], we need to agree on what words we'll use and what those words mean.

This isn't just for this class. All scholars must know the vocabulary of their discipline. A "discipline" is an area of study, and people who study that area seriously are called "disciplinarians."

We are disciplinarians, too.

On a scale of one to five, five being most important and one being not at all important, how important do you think the Language of the Discipline is to being successful in what you are studying?

[Either discuss or (preferred) have students line up in the order of importance they choose, with one side of the classroom being a one and the other side being a five.]

A famous American author named James Michener wrote novels about places and their history. One of the places he wrote about was the Chesapeake Bay near Washington, D.C.

[If you have a map, show where Chesapeake Bay is.]

In the novel, Michener described how a man felt who wanted desperately to be a boat builder but was held back because he didn't know the vocabulary of the discipline.

[Using a document camera or a Smart Board, display the quote below. Two versions of the quote are provided, one with unfamiliar words defined and one without. Use whichever you prefer, or show the one with definitions first, and then re-read without definitions.]

Think back to our scale of one to five about the importance of academic vocabulary. How important do you think this carpenter thinks the language of the discipline is?

[Either discuss or (preferred) have students line up in the order of importance they choose, with one side of the classroom being a one and the other side being a five.]

To help us share our ideas in this class, we'll be learning the Language of the Discipline. Whenever you see this image (show icon), you will know, "Oh, we're talking about the words and tools that people use to talk about [insert content]."

Michener quote with some words explained:

"But always he lacked the essential tool without which the workman can never attain (reach) true mastery: he did not know the names of any of the parts he was building, and without the name he was artistically incomplete. It was not by accident that doctors and lawyers and butchers invented specific but secret names for the things they did; to possess the name was to know the secret. With correct names one entered into a new world of proficiency (expertise), became the member of an arcane (mysterious or secret) brotherhood, a sharer of mysteries, and in the end a performer of merit. Without the names one remained a bumbler (someone who makes mistakes because they don't know) or, in the case of boatbuilding, a mere carpenter." James Michener, *Chesapeake*

Michener quote with no explanation:

"But always he lacked the essential tool without which the workman can never attain true mastery: he did not know the names of any of the parts he was building, and without the name he was artistically incomplete. It was not by accident that doctors and lawyers and butchers invented specific but secret names for the things they did; to possess the name was to know the secret. With correct names one entered into a new world of proficiency, became the member of an arcane brotherhood, a sharer of mysteries, and in the end a performer of merit. Without the names one remained a bumbler or, in the case of boatbuilding, a mere carpenter." James Michener, *Chesapeake*

What Are Some Sample Question Stems?

Low Level Questions (Beware!)

- What is the Language of this Discipline?
- Define this Language of the Discipline.

Apply

- Give an example of _____.
- What/who is this and why should you care?

Analysis

- Describe the difference between _____ and _____. Draft two versions of your explanation: one for your teacher, one for your classmate.
- Explain the difference between [this word] and [that word]?
- What words do you notice that aren't words you use, but you can still understand their meaning?

Evaluate

- What are synonyms for _____, and why are they more or less accurate than _____?
- How important is the understanding of the term ____ to being able to ____ [insert task or skill]?
- Which words support/argue against the idea that _____?
- What are three most important words you would need to describe this?

Synthesize

- What words would a [insert discipline] use to describe this?
- What would happen if [some word] were taken out of the problem/sentence?
- In what way did a misunderstanding of [this word] lead to conflict?
- How would you explain [some word] to someone who didn't understand this concept?

- If you couldn't use the word _____, what would be a word you could use to describe _____?

What Are Some Sample Uses?

You're probably already using Language of the Discipline without calling it that. Any vocabulary exercise, any discussion of a tool, any learning of an acronym...all of these are Language of the Discipline opportunities.

Whenever students are considering something deeply, they must understand and use with precision the Language of the Discipline. Consider this discussion question in a science class: "Is air matter?" In class, we'll definitely look at Rules and Details, but we need Language of the Discipline in order to truly consider it. Whether it is simply a discussion or a more formalized activity like a graphic organizer or some other product piece, the integration of Language of the Discipline is a core part of understanding content more deeply.

Sometimes, you'll use Language of the Discipline to help students arrive at a deeper idea. For example, in the short story "The Ravine" by Gram Salisbury, a teacher may use a word from the story and challenge thinking with it, saying something like, "A '*haole*' is a non-native Hawaiian – a white person. What does calling Starlene a *haole* tell us about the other characters?" In general, analyzing the words used by characters and historical figures is a key to character analysis. You can take it a step further by having students suggest synonyms and then evaluating the effect of that.

In math, we may challenge students to consider the difference between definitions (Language of the Discipline), and Rules. Consider: In mathematics, a function is a relationship between a set of inputs and a set of outputs. Each input has exactly one output. Are these statements definitions or rules? Can a rule also be a definition?

In general, science and math teachers could use more Language of the Discipline activities than they may be used to or that their textbook provides. Some common activities include word webs, word ladders, crosswords, fill-in-the blank, and even pronunciation helps ("Axes [plural of the tool ax or axe] is pronounced 'Ack-sizz', but in math, 'Axes' [plural of axis] is pronounced 'Ack-seas'." Which sounds cooler to you? The tool word or the math word? Let's vote!"

Etymology can be a strong strategy in content areas other than language arts, but it's underused. Here's an example from math: "The word 'integer' is from the Latin *in-* 'not' + the root *tangere* 'to touch.' It means 'whole' or 'untouched.' Why is this a good name for this set of numbers?"

Teachers can use the Language of the Discipline element to cue students that this is a key word, label anchor charts or KWL charts, open up a discussion about a new topic by introducing unfamiliar vocabulary, or a host of other ideas. A simple example of its use would be a high school biology teacher who might have a diagram of a cell that students are to label. The teacher could put a Language of the Discipline icon on the diagram to signal students that they're going to use the formal academic vocabulary to label the diagram.

The same element could be used differently with the same content, taking advanced students deeper. Instead of labeling the diagram, students could categorize the words related to the cell's structure and then research the etymology of those words. In this instance, nucleus, nucleolus, and nuclear membrane all arise from the Latin *nux*, meaning "kernel" or "inner part."

To deepen this exercise, combine it with Multiple Perspectives. The teacher could ask students to make a chart with the name scientists have given the parts of the cell in one column, then create another column with what political scientists might call that same structure, and yet another column with what the cell itself might call the structure.

We can ask students to confront vocabulary. Is "cartel" always negative? How is "safe" different in lab safety than in baseball? How are they the same? In a design class, a teacher may ask, "How is the word 'constraint' different in design than it is in math? Do you think it leads to greater creativity in design than it does in math? What about in writing?"

You can ask students to think of three words in the problem that are the most likely to be misunderstood. Choose one and write a definition for it that you think will be most likely to help someone who has never heard of that word understand it. Give your definition to a friend without telling him/her the word and have him/her guess the word and rate your definition on a scale of 1 - 10.

An activity we like to do is to have students interview a word. Consider the word "conflict." This is a word commonly encountered in both language arts and social studies. Students "interview" the word by writing or recording responses to questions as if they were that word. Here are some suggestions:

- What words mean the same as you?
- What makes you happy?
- Who or what is your best friend?
- What do you dislike most?
- If you could give anyone advice, who would you give it to, and what would you say?

Consider that you could ask these same questions of virtually any word in any content area. Students can interview latitude, measurement, even, organic, complementary (as in colors), and on and on.

For high ability students in particular, playing with words is often really fun. Consider in a Spanish class that students could be given this task sequence:

- Change "tengo" to first person plural.
- Write three nouns that begin with the fifth letter of the new conjugation.

- Write an acrostic poem with one of the nouns using at least one verb, one noun, and one adjective.

This exercise is a good example of how you can integrate Language of the Discipline with content exercises. It doesn't have to be a separate, "Let's stop everything and work on vocabulary!" Language of the Discipline is far more flexible than that.

6

RULES

ONE OF THE MOST EXCITING THINGS about working with the Rules element is how much broader it is than most students expect when they hear the word "rule." They think it will be a bunch of thou-shalt-nots, when Rules are far more complex and engaging than simple prohibitions. When Rules are broken, there are negative consequences of some sort, but that gets far more complicated than classroom expectations.

Rules: What It Must Do

The Rules prompt encompasses laws, expectations, standards, methods, and other "required" aspects of a field. Breaking a Rule leads to consequences. When students think through the filter of "what is required or expected," they learn to think within a system. This brings them closer to how an expert thinks. When an engineer approaches a problem, they use their familiarity with Rules to design within constraints. A designer of clothes knows how each type of fabric behaves, allowing them to develop interesting new ideas by working with those Rules.

Novices do not know the intricate Rules of a system so their ideas can be impractical or even impossible. As a teacher, you've probably heard someone give their simple solution to education that could never actually work. "All the schools need to do is..." Sorry if we just made your blood pressure go up. A person who does not know the Rules is limited in their ability to think about the subject.

Rules: This, Not That

If you're defining Rules too narrowly, you're leaving a lot on the table. If you only think of formal rules like classroom rules, school rules, or laws, then you can expand the meaning to include anything that should be followed or that leads to a consequence if broken.

We also see folks defining Rules as things that "cannot be broken" or that "must be followed." You *can* break many Rules. In fact, if you carefully weigh the consequences, breaking a Rule might even be the best choice. Some of the most admired people in history have purposefully broken rules. Consider asking the question: "What happens when this Rule breaks?"

Finally, if all you do is ask students to "list the rules," make sure to build towards higher-order thinking and towards other prompts:

- Not just: List the Rules of the scientific method.

- Move towards: Which Rules of the scientific method do you think are most difficult to follow?
- Or: What are the Ethical consequences of skipping a Rule of the scientific method?

What Else Does This Element Include?

The Rules element encompasses five different categories (and probably even more!). The first of these is standards. Standards aren't just content standards like the Common Core. They're standards such as in weights and measures. You can't simply decide a pound is now twenty ounces instead of sixteen (Although that would be fun if you were trying to lose weight! Instant weight loss!). There are standards of what a product has to have to be called "organic" or even "mayonnaise." There are standards of how many fly parts can be in peanut butter, and most of us teach content where there are standards agreed upon within our discipline, even if they are not as interesting (or gross) as fly parts in peanut butter.

Rules also include directions. You can ignore your GPS and go whatever way you want, but it's possible that if you don't follow the directions, you will end up either someplace you didn't want to go or it will take you longer to get there. There is typically a penalty for not following directions correctly, and that is why it is a Rule.

Closely related to directions is methods. The scientific method is a Rule. I mean, it doesn't impress me if you create your hypotheses after the experiment has ended. Just recently, Lisa inadvertently ignored the directions in a recipe for banana bread, throwing everything willy-nilly into her beloved cobalt blue mixer only to find that the texture was all wrong. It really does matter if you cream the butter and sugar, add the eggs one at a time, and mix in the flour one cup at a time. Who knew? Well, the Rules element knew. Methods are Rules because when they are not followed, we don't get the result we were looking for.

Organization may not seem like a Rule, but it is. From something as simple as the way books are supposed to be returned to your shelves or names put on papers, to something as complicated as animal classification (Kingdom, Phylum, Class, Order, Family, Genus, Species, etc.), organization is an important part of the Rules element. It would cause great confusion if a botanist decided that she were going to start calling a Red Maple tree a *rubrum Acer* rather than *Acer rubrum*. The nomenclature is part of the organization, and that organization is a Rule. We see this in the set up of problems in math, the structure of governments in social studies, family organizations in sociology, the hierarchies in corporations and social groups, and on and on. It's possible that organization will be the aspect of this element your students interface with most.

The last aspect of Rules is usual behavior, and this is a favorite because there is so much room for interesting conversations that deepen both reasoning skills and content mastery. For example, if a character usually behaves one way in response to another character, and then suddenly behaves a different way, how do/will other characters respond? How do certain molecules or atoms or planets or numbers usually behave?

What Are Some Sample Question Stems?

Low Level Questions (Beware!)

- What are the rules in _____?
- List the rules.

Apply

- What restrictions would you add to or take away from the rule?
- What rules do even numbers follow when you add them?

Analyze

- Does everyone/everything act the way ____ does?
- What has to happen in order for

  _____ to occur/happen/work well?

Evaluate

- Why is this rule necessary?
- Which steps are the most important to follow in this problem?
- How effective is this rule?
- What does this rule ask you to believe?
- Who/what is most likely to break this rule?

- Can you clarify the difference between these two methods? Which is more likely to achieve the desired result?
- Predict what would happen if no one/everyone followed this rule?
- How does ____ usually behave? What is likely to cause a change in that usual behavior?
- How did the breaking of the rule change the way ____ happened? Was this a good change or a bad one in the long run?

Synthesize

- In what ways is this rule misunderstood? Who is most likely to misunderstand it?
- Give an example of this rule in another domain (i.e., what would it look like in another experiment/story/problem?)
- Can you defend the position of the person/thing that disrupted the system/event/process?
- How would you explain the character's resistance to the hierarchy of the family?
- How much change would there be if the directions were not followed?
- What happens if this organizational structure breaks down?
- Come up with a better rule.
- Defend the position of the person who created this rule.

What Are Some Sample Uses?

Perhaps the most simple of Rules activities involve identification of Rules. We can stay at this level for a very long time, listing the Rules of spiders (must have eight legs, must have a web, must have two body segments, etc.). We can make these a little more interesting by adding in some analysis. Which of the Rules the character set for him/herself were most helpful to the character? Part of what makes working with Rules so rewarding is that it seems like it lends itself to the lowest levels of Bloom's, yet so readily marches its way up the pyramid.

Consider a progression like this:

- List the Rules of the U.S. Constitution.
- Contrast the Rules of the U.S. Constitution with those of another country.
- Apply the Rules of Japan's constitution to the US. What would it be like?
- Judge which Rules of the U.S. Constitution are least fair.
- Create the Rules for a new constitution.

Resist the temptation to leave Rules languishing at the base of the pyramid of thinking skills.

Giving students examples of broken rules and asking them to fix them is a simple exercise, yet often feels much more like a puzzle than simply solving a problem would. For example, instead of asking, "How would you write the number '100' in Roman numerals?", a teacher could show "VV" and ask, "What Rule of Roman numerals is this breaking?"

A teacher could also give a number of examples and ask students to infer a Rule from them. This works even if the students have not been taught the Rule explicitly before.

All math is solved with Patterns and Rules. If students are getting answers incorrect or not arriving at an answer at all, often it is ignorance of Rules that is getting in the way.

Rules can be used for creative constraint, which is what we call the practice of giving students constraints or boundaries for the purpose of forcing them into a creative process. We can require students to write sentences using specific syntactical structures (syntax is a Rule) such as "You need to use at least two complex sentences, and one needs to begin with an appositive phrase." In math, we might say, "Create a 6-digit number that has at least one even digit, one digit that is able to be skip counted by three, and the number must end with a digit that is prime."

In science, nomenclature bridges both Rules and Language of the Discipline. Yes, the words we use for the scientific names of things are academic vocabulary, but they are also governed by Rules. I can't decide that I'm going to call animals by their species name, followed by the phylum. I have to go in the prescribed order. Likewise, chemical compounds have rules that govern their names. A teacher can give incorrect names and ask them to be corrected ("I say NaClO is sodium hyperchloride. Fix it.") or I can give a student a compound with the elements mixed up and say,

"Rewrite this in Hill System order." I can ask students to create an entirely new compound and name that compound following standard naming conventions.

Remember to consider usual behavior as an aspect of Rules. This can lead to subtle, wonderful analysis. Consider this brief passage from the short story, "The Ravine":

> When Vinny and three others dropped down into the ravine, they entered a jungle thick with tangled trees and rumors of what might have happened to the dead boy's body.

You could frame a lovely Rules-based question around this by saying something like, "Usually it's vines that are tangled in a jungle, not trees. In what way does this make it different/make it more creepy/set the mood/serve as foreshadowing?"

Rules can also be used to give students a hint that there is a problem, while still allowing them space to self-correct. I may sketch out the icon I'm using for Rules next to a broken rule (such as incorrect comma placement, missed Order of Operations step, etc.), without identifying exactly what is wrong.

The key to effective activities with Rules is to keep its nuances in mind. Rules is an easy element to take to high levels of thinking very quickly, in part because students are familiar with the concept of the element in a different and deeper way that with others (Unanswered Questions, for example, is less familiar and needs more practice) because they've been hearing them all of their lives. Leverage this to your advantage. Rules will likely be an element you lean on again and again to generate and encourage critical thinking.

How Do I Introduce It to Students?

Playing the "What Am I?" Game is a favorite way to introduce the Rules element to students. To play, ask students to answer the question, "What am I?" about a list of statements. All of the statements are rules about a certain thing or activity. Here are some examples:

What am I?

- I have to have three sides.
- I have to have three angles.
- If one of my angles is ninety degrees, I'm right.
- The sum of my interior angles is 180 degrees.

What am I?

- Always wear your seatbelt.
- Obey the speed limit.
- You must have a license.
- Signal 100 feet before a turn.
- Yield to pedestrians.

What am I?

- "I" before "E" except after "C".
- Use the possessive in front of a gerund.

- Sentences begin with a capital letter.
- Some pronouns are already possessive and need no apostrophe.

What am I?

- Waft, don't inhale.
- Do not return unused chemicals to their original container.
- Tie back long hair.
- Never look into a container that is being heated.

You will need to choose examples that your students will be familiar with, although it is fine if they don't immediately recognize or know all of the examples you show. It's most fun to play several rounds. You can have students work in groups to come up with their own examples and play a few rounds of those suggestions.

You can also describe a situation and ask for the rules of it. For example, what are the rules of standing in a line?

Explain the different aspects of the Rules element that we discussed above (standards, directions, etc.), using examples such as:

- What would happen if I decided that you now needed a 97 to get an "A" in this class? What would happen if I decided that a foot was now ten inches instead of twelve? (standards)

- What would happen if I decided to drive on whatever side of the road I felt like? What if I started saying "left" whenever I meant "right"? (directions)

- What would happen if I decided to brush my teeth only right before I ate and never after? What would happen if I rinsed out my hair, then put conditioner on it, and then dried it? (methods)

- What if every morning when you woke up, everything in your house was in a different place – your toothbrush was in the garage, your food was in the bathroom, your clothes were by the front door? What would happen if every day when school ended, you had no idea how you were getting home? (Note: This one is an all-too-often reality, especially early in the year!) What would happen if the librarian decided to arrange all of the books by binding color rather than by author or topic? (organization)

Explain that all of these are things we consider when we use the Rules element, and they exist to make things work better, more effectively, or to help people enjoy things more.

Sometimes we use the example of Monopoly®. If you don't like playing Monopoly, it's highly likely you're playing it wrong. Most people complain that games last too long, yet the reason they last so long is that people play "house rules" that lengthen the game. Two common ones are to put money in the middle of the board when people have to pay fines and then giving that money to a person who lands on Free Parking. Friends, that's not the rule, and it keeps broke people in the game far too long.

Another common error is to forget to auction property. In the actual rules, when someone lands on an unowned property, that property will be purchased. If the person who lands on it doesn't want to purchase it for the stated price, then the property goes up for auction and any player, including the player who just declined to buy it at full price, may bid on it. It might sell for $5, and that's fine. When you play by this rule, the game goes much more quickly because the property is all sold after very few trips around the board.

The bottom line is that if you don't like something, it's possible you're playing it all wrong. School is like that for many students. They don't like it because they're playing it all wrong. What a great discussion that would be! In what way is a school a game, and how do you play it incorrectly?

7

PATTERNS

MUCH LIKE BIG IDEA AND DETAILS work well to defined each other, the contrast between Patterns and Rules can help students to understand each prompt better. Rules *have* to happen. They must be followed, or there are consequences. Rules might take the form of requirements, hierarchies, or expectations. On the other hand, Patterns are repeating ideas that do not have to continue repeating. In fact, the most interesting moment is often when a pattern fails.

Patterns: What it Must Do

Patterns involve repetition and prediction. The Patterns element must invite students to consider the many ways in which things repeat and cycle, and then to use that information to make their own predictions. In order to be effective, teachers must not allow students to stop at merely identifying patterns, but rather make sure that they analyze and evaluate them. The patterns they observe and detect must be used to predict future events, be compared to other similar and dissimilar patterns, and be analyzed to determine their importance and value.

You may be noticing a pattern here (no pun intended). With Depth and Complexity, it's all about the thinking that students are doing. We use Depth and Complexity to raise thinking level. Just recognizing the existence of a place to use an element is insufficient. We must make that recognition useful.

Patterns: This, Not That

Because Patterns asks students to go beyond recognitions alone, we must ask students questions that go beyond merely identifying Patterns. If you're only asking for identification of a pattern, you're not using this element correctly.

- This: Why is it important to understand this pattern?
- Not (Only) This: What is the life cycle of the butterfly?

- This: What will happen eventually if we keep following the pattern of these numbers?
- Not (Only) This: What is the pattern of these numbers?

- This: Who most desperately needs this pattern to break?
- Not (Only) This: How could this pattern break?

The confusion of Patterns and Rules is the other common mistake we see with this element. We'll see someone consider something like the Order of Operations and think, "Is that Patterns or Rules?" A simple litmus test works well: if it isn't followed, does it lead to something interesting or something unpleasant/awkward/wrong? With Order of Operations, if it's not followed, it leads (quite often) to incorrect answers; therefore, it's ultimately a Rule.

Often, this confusion occurs when students are looking at the most basic idea of Rules. It's less common when they're considering Rules as usual behavior or standards. Those applications are typically more obvious.

Patterns can nest within Rules, so it isn't superficial analysis. That's part of what makes Depth and Complexity effective. If it were easy to see something and respond quickly, "Oh! That's such-and-such," we'd have some very shallow thinking. Inviting students to consider if something is a Pattern or a Rule is one of the simplest, yet quite effective, activities one can do with the element.

Sometimes Patterns lead us to Rules, such as with functions in mathematics. As students work with functions and see that a certain input leads to a certain output, they can put those Patterns together to create a Rule.

At the end of the day, it doesn't really matter if we get the element "right" or "wrong." What matters is that we're using the thinking skill to deepen and develop our students' analytical skills. If our students walk out of class thinking, "I *still* think that was a Rule," then we've had a successful thinking day.

What are Some Sample Question Stems?

Apply

- How can we predict what will happen next based on what has happened so far?
- Can you condense this Pattern into a single sentence?
- Who is most likely to be familiar with this Pattern?
- What factors led to the establishment of these factors?

Analyze

- In what ways is this Pattern the same as ____ Pattern? In what ways is it different? How important are those differences?
- What things does the Pattern ask us to assume?
- How can you explain what must have happened when ____?
- In what way do you think this Pattern is somewhat Rule-like?
- How are these things/elements/ideas/characters connected to each other?

Evaluate

- Which of the recurring events do you see as negative? Positive? Most likely to lead to change?
- Why do you think these elements/ideas/events/etc. are repeated time and time again?

- Is it possible to have a different result if we follow the Pattern exactly?
- Would everyone agree on the value of this Pattern to ___?

Synthesize

- Predict what would happen if this part of the cycle was altered.
- What would happen if we changed the order in which _____ occurred?
- How would you explain this Pattern to someone who had never heard of it?
- Why would someone want to break this Pattern?

What are Some Sample Uses?

Patterns are everywhere, so this will be a commonly used element in most domains. There are some very general activities with Patterns virtually all teachers can use.

In fact, we can't think of a single content area that is not chock-full of Patterns. From tessellations in mathematics, to plot and archetype in language arts, from migration in social studies to life/water/plant/rock cycles in science, or from verb conjugation in world languages to the patterns in music measures, our content is full of beautiful patterns waiting to be discovered and analyzed.

If you teach language arts, Patterns will be your constant friend. The common plot diagram itself is a Pattern. The backstory sets up the current Pattern (the three little pigs live with their mom in a house). The inciting incident breaks that Pattern and sets the story in motion. Remember how when Patterns break, interesting things happen? In language arts, when the Pattern breaks, stories unfold. The rest of the story (rising action, climax, falling action, resolution) exists as characters attempt to discover and establish a new Pattern.

In social studies, particularly history and government, we see Pattern in the cycle of conflict-war-peace. Often, within that peace lie the seeds of the next conflict, such as with the Treaty of Versailles. Etymology is Patterns, so if you're looking at vocabulary, you cannot help but approach it through the lens of root words and prefixes/suffixes. These are Patterns.

Really, it's hard to stop giving examples because this element is so common. Alongside Language of the Discipline and Details, it is perhaps the element that virtually every teacher can use with regularity. Consider that all math problems are solved with Patterns and Rules. All stories are Patterns, as described above. Because it is human nature to seek out and even impose Patterns, this will very likely be a commonly used element in your classroom.

If you'd like some book recommendations, we love *Patterns in Nature: Why the Natural World Looks the Way It Does* by Phillip Ball. Also, there is a wide variety of books available in many content areas, from *The Tiny Seed* by Eric Carle for as young as Pre-K to the one above for teens and adults. If you're a math teacher, *Growing Patterns: Fibonacci Numbers in Nature* by Sarah C. Campbell is a great choice.

What are Some Specific Examples?

Students can:

- Detect and describe Patterns
- Evaluate the Pattern's importance
- Compare one Pattern to another Pattern
- Identify primary and secondary Patterns
- Recognize when and where a Pattern breaks and the effect of that break
- See the Pattern out of order and correct it

Just these simple ideas combined with the sample question stems above should get you off to a good start using Patterns in your classroom.

You can have students really work a Pattern through a progression of tasks. They could sketch out the life cycle of the butterfly and analyze the Pattern to determine at what part of the cycle they feel the developing butterfly is most vulnerable. They could then consider at what stage it is most free. To differentiate for high ability learners, you could have them redesign the life cycle of the butterfly to make it less vulnerable.

Patterns is useful for exploring quadrilaterals (What patterns do we see across different quadrilaterals? What patterns break between certain quadrilaterals?) and can lead to formalized rules about those shapes (There is a pattern of parallel lines amongst squares, rectangles, rhombi, and parallelograms, but squares and rectangles *must* have 90° angles.).

You can use Patterns to set up classroom activities. For example, if students are going to be working with a small group or shoulder partner, then alone, then back in the group/with the partner, that's a pattern. Using that language ("Here's the pattern for our activity today") helps students create a schema in their mind that may lead to better classroom management of the activity.

When you're teaching tested subjects, helping students see and understand the patterns in the test is essential. What types of questions exist? What are common elements in the different types of questions? How long should be spent on a typical problem of that question type? When students have tests returned, they can look for patterns in the types of questions missed.

Any kind of sorting is a Pattern, so students may sort words into groups (-am words, words with three syllables, etc.), sort numbers into sets, or sort characters into types. These are all examples of Patterns.

Lisa particularly loves using sociograms – visual representations of the way characters, people, numbers, or things are connected with one another. Sociograms are typically used with language arts, but it's not limited to them. Giving students a set of numbers and asking them to come up with a pattern that connects them or giving them a list of planets and asking them to connect them leads to deep analysis. It's like a content exercise of the old game "Six Degrees of Kevin Bacon."

Here's a math sociogram Lisa uses to have students connect numbers:'

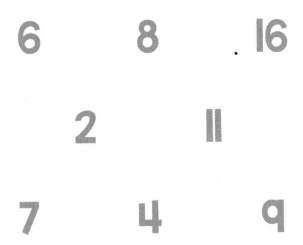

When students work on it, it begins to look like this:

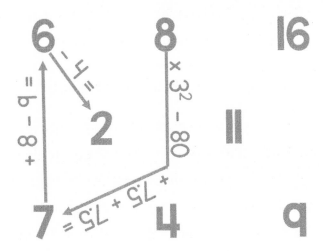

Here's a sociogram Lisa has students complete for the novel *The Cricket in Times Square.*

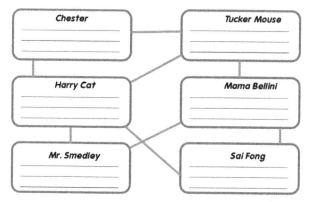

List three traits of each character and then show how that character is connected to the character(s) with whom they share connectors.

If you teach mathematics, you must use Patterns and Rules – they are the foundation of how all math problems are solved. If you teach anything else, you will find that once students are alerted to the idea of Patterns, they will discover them again and again, sometimes surprising you with their insight. Pattern recognition itself is a skill (It's actually an IQ subtest on many tests of intelligence), and we can build this skill in students.

How do I Introduce It to Students?

Patterns lends itself to a variety of introductory methods. It's useful to introduce Rules and Patterns using a simple discussion of the school day. There are rules that must be followed (recess and lunch breaks, playground rules, due dates, end of year tests) and there are patterns that repeat, but sometimes break (assemblies disrupt daily schedules, music class is skipped due to a holiday, minimum days change dismissal times, and sometimes we have a substitute teacher).

Ian enjoys using *The Giving Tree* as content to introduce Rules and Patterns because the story is full of them. The Tree *always* calls The Boy "Boy" (even when he's an old man). The Boy *usually* comes and goes... until he doesn't. In the end he stays, sitting on the stump. This suddenly broken pattern is an important moment to discuss.

Lisa introduces Patterns in a couple of ways. She'll sometimes show a picture of a triceratops dinosaur and tell students, "Patterns is why we're still drinking dinosaur pee." A lively discussion of the water cycle ensues (along with the occasional parent email!) that allows for an understanding of the idea of Patterns as things that repeat or have recurring elements.

Sometimes, she'll use predictive text, such as *The Three Little Pigs* that allows the students to fill in repetitive phrases ("not by the hair of my chinny-chin-chin...").

With all of these ideas, it's then important to bring out the idea that with Patterns:

- Things can be repeated
- You can often predict what comes next
- When you see repetition, look for the Pattern
- Patterns can be man-made or natural
- A recurring element can be a Pattern

You may wish to use a combination of these ideas to emphasize different aspects of Pattern. There is no rule (see what we did there?) that you can only introduce students to an element one time in one experience. Short, different introductions can work well, giving you the chance to remind students of what was discussed before or even to capture those students who may have been absent when it was introduced.

8

UNANSWERED QUESTIONS

UNANSWERED QUESTIONS IS THE ELEMENT of mysterious beauty in our content. British physicist Brian Cox once said, "I'm comfortable with the unknown—that's the point of science. There are places out there, billions of places out there, that we know nothing about. And the fact that we know nothing about them excites me, and I want to go out and find out about them. And that's what science is. So I think if you're not comfortable with the unknown, then it's difficult to be a scientist... I don't need an answer. I don't need answers to everything. I want to have answers to find." Unanswered Questions helps us awaken this kind of mindset within our students.

Unanswered Questions: What It Must Do

Unanswered Questions asks three main questions:

1. What do you not know the answer to because that answer is unavailable?

2. What do you not know the answer to, but you could find out with currently available knowledge or resources?

3. What do you know the answer to, but others may disagree with you?

It must dive deeply into the unknown, and it must always consider available resources.

Unanswered Questions: This, Not That

If you're using Unanswered Questions as a way to ask students what they still want to learn, you're not doing it right. Along with Big Idea, this is the most commonly misused element. Unanswered Questions is not an abbreviated KWL chart, simply asking students, "What do you still want to know?" Let's be honest: That question rarely elicits quality responses.

Unanswered Questions should not just be a prompt we put at the end of a worksheet, telling students to "List three questions you have."

As teachers, we can't just rely on students to give us *their* Unanswered Questions. Often, students simply do not know enough to ask great questions (that's why they're the students!). We should use this prompt to supply students with fascinating Unanswered Questions which get them wondering.

When working with Unanswered Questions, stay focused on variations of the theme of the questions we listed above:

1. What do you not know the answer to because that answer is unavailable?

2. What do you not know the answer to, but you could find out with currently available knowledge or resources?

3. What do you know the answer to, but others may disagree with you about?

We rarely build curiosity with the question, "What do you still want to know?" because it is far too easy to simply answer, "Nothing." Rather, we can and should explore more deeply into the realms of available knowledge and resources.

> This: Imagine a resource that would answer this question. Who is more likely to have it or to be able to find it?
> Not This: What would you still like to know about it?

> This: Why did these scientists decide that they had reached a reasonable conclusion, even though it later turned out to be incorrect?
> Not This: What did the scientists decide?

The key to using this element correctly is to remember what it explores. It looks at things that are uncertain, things that are ambiguous, things that are doubtful, things that have resource or knowledge gaps, and conclusions that people disagree with.

This doesn't mean everything related to this element is straight out of an episode of *Unsolved Mysteries*. Rather, it means that we are helping students grow comfortable with not knowing. It means helping students accept that some things will never be known or agreed upon. It means asking questions that can't be answered by saying, "Alexa...."

What Else Does This Element Include?

It includes unsolved mysteries, conundrums, puzzles, things that are doubtful, and things that are ambiguous. Dilemmas fall into this element. For instance, if we keep gorillas in zoos, it's not great for those gorillas, but if we don't keep gorillas in zoos, people won't care about gorillas in the wild because they won't see them. Sometimes we know the answer for one area or circumstance, but not another. For example, I know that a common breakfast food in the United States is cereal, but I don't know what common breakfast foods are in Argentina.

Things that are lacking in certainty fall into this element as well. When President Kennedy was facing off with Nikita Krushchev during the Cuban Missile Crisis, the outcome was uncertain. That's an Unanswered Question. Discrepancies that occur when we expect one result but get another are also a part of this element. For example, the difference between a hypothesis and what really happened is an Unanswered Question. Wherever there is a lab, wherever there is a research project, there will always be an Unanswered Question.

Anytime we're asking a student to make a prediction or do research, we're looking at Unanswered Questions. This leads students closer towards a level of comfort with ambiguity and an attitude of curiosity. Especially for high ability students, getting them to be more comfortable with ambiguity is critical, and this is the element that does that best. It is a key factor in becoming a Disciplinarian (see Chapter 20) because Disciplinarians are comfortable not knowing everything in their field. Brian Cox said, "You dig deeper and it gets more and more complicated, and you get confused, and it's tricky, and it's hard, but...it is beautiful." This element asks our students to become comfortable with the idea that the more they know, the more they realize they don't know, and that's fine (even beautiful).

Unanswered Questions guide exploration from known to unknown content, asking students to consider, "What do I know now? What do I need/want to know? How do I find out?" All research should be guided by an Unanswered Question. If it's not, it's not research; it's a report. To do this, we have to constantly be focused on the quality and availability of resources. We have to help students ask, "What resources are most likely to answer this question, and where can I find them? Are these resources reliable?" Always circle back to available resources. This doesn't have to mean a trip to the library. The text is a resource. The data from a lab is a resource. The idea of "resource" is much broader than websites and books, although these are definitely essential.

What Are Some Sample Question Stems?

Apply

- How does using a graph/array/etc. clarify this problem?
- What resources do you need to help you answer these questions?
- Is this fact or fiction? How do you know?

Analyze

- Who else had this question? How did they answer it? How could this help us?

- What other already answered questions relate to this one?

- What information would have been most helpful to ___ at this point?

- How are the resources we're using to solve this today different from the resources used in the past?

Evaluate

- How important is it that this question be answered?

- How credible is this source?

- What information is incomplete?

- What is still uncertain about ___?

- Of all of the choices, which seems most likely?

- What would we need to know to be able to answer this question?

- What do the characters not understand?

Synthesize

- What are some possible unintended consequences of ___?

- What questions did I/you not ask that I/you should have?

- What would have to happen or change to make the character more/less this way/that way?

- What new questions does the solving of this problem create?
- If so-and-so hadn't done such-and-such, what is one thing that would be different in today's world?
- What might happen if ____ were solved/answered?
- How can you explain the difference between your hypothesis and your results?
- If you were ____ and could have one Unanswered Question answered, what would it be?
- How can you explain the discrepancy between your hypothesis and your results?
- Think of three positive consequences if ____ had happened.
- Let's come up with at least ____ possibilities for what might have happened.
- If you reversed ____ and ____, would it still be ____? Explain how you know.
- How might ____ or ____ affect ____?

What Are Some Sample Uses?

Although we listed lots of question stems above, the value of Unanswered Questions in questioning is worthy of a mention here as well. Even very young students can consider excellent quality questions with this element. Consider these questions from a first grade class:

- What do plants do to spread seeds when there aren't enough birds?
- What would make a bird eat one seed over another?
- Which do you think came first, ice or water?
- What holiday do you think is the favorite of this character?
- What does the character own that you think is the most important thing to him/her?
- If moons are important, why don't all planets have them? Would you rather live on a planet with zero, one, or many moons?

Here are some examples for older students:

- What would happen if a number line were not a straight line?
- Why do some bodies of water get polluted while others don't?
- Which is more valuable to animals, a river or a lake?
- Which step do you think is the genesis of the water cycle?

The questions don't need to be solely content based. We can use this element for self-reflection as well. What factors do you think will influence your work this grading period?

As we already mentioned, all research should be guided by an Unanswered Question. Teachers can give the Unanswered Question (most likely to be needed in early grades) or ask students to develop their own. You may need to begin by giving them the guiding Unanswered Question and then helping them move toward developing their own. If you teach a lab science or if students are doing labs in your class, Unanswered Questions will guide those labs as well.

Branching out beyond questions, labs, and research, other activities that work perfectly with this element include mock trials, Socratic Seminars, Philosophical Chairs or other collaborative learning strategies. You can have students create products of varying complexity to represent their thinking. For example, they can make quick movies or share in an online collaborative document.

Working with Unanswered Questions is rewarding for students and teachers. As you practice developing questions that leave room for student wonder, you will get better at creating those questions, and your students will get better at answering them with reasoned consideration born of deep curiosity, and they will begin to develop their own.

How Do I Introduce It to Students?

Show students images of things that are still mysteries, such as Amelia Earhart's disappearance, the building of Stonehenge, the ghost ship *Mary Celeste*, the lost colony of Roanoke, etc. Ask them what they think may have happened. If they're unfamiliar with the stories, give them a one- or two-sentence soundbite. Explain that the world is full of questions and mysteries that remain unanswered. Some are waiting for new information to come to light, while others will probably never be known. Sometimes we only have to wait until the next episode of the show or the next book in the series, and sometimes we wait decades or centuries or even forever.

Not all of these are mysteries like you would see on television. They are questions about what we know and what we can never know. For instance, according to the laws of physics, there should be an equal amount of matter and anti-matter in the universe, and yet there is way more matter. The Millennium Prize Problems in mathematics are a set of seven problems set out in the year 2000, and to date, only one has been solved. Why do humans tell stories? How does the Earth's interior work and how does that affect the surface? Even songs we listen to have unanswered questions. Who let the dogs out, anyway?

Divide the students into groups of three or four. Give each group a die. Display the following so all students can see it:

1. What is a question that you don't know the answer to?
2. Where is a place you go to find answers to questions?
3. What is something that you think that sometimes people don't agree with you about? (A great food? A great song?)
4. What do you think happened to the *Mary Celeste*? (or other mystery)
5. What is something people sometimes think about you, but it isn't correct?

6. If you could have one question about your future answered, what would it be?

If you can, show each face of the die along with these instructions, but if not, the numerals 1 through 6 will work.

Have students take turns rolling the die and responding to the corresponding question. It's fine if they roll the same roll as another student because the answers are individual.

Gather them back and explain that when we look at our learning through the lens of Unanswered Questions, we're looking at these kinds of things (see the list above). Share with them that this element will help us become more comfortable with the idea that there are different ways of finding things out, different lengths of time it will take to find things out, and different questions we all have that we want to research the answers to. If your students are old enough, you may wish to share one or both of the Brian Cox quotes. End with the idea that in this element there is a little bit of magic. There will also be the possibility of a surprise, and that makes it truly fun.

9

TRENDS

IAN WOULD LIKE TO VOTE Trends off the island, while Lisa loves it. Should make for an interesting chapter.

Trends: What It Must Do

Trends is the lens through which we examine the direction things or people are moving, developing, and changing and what forces are acting on that change. It must ask, "In what way is this data moving, and why?" Trends is the cause and effect element. If you're asking students to analyze cause and effect, Trends is your friend to end all friends. Unlike Change over Time, it is not necessarily time dependent.

Trends: This not That

If you're ignoring Trends all together, you're doing it all wrong. If you're not using Trends, you're probably force-fitting another element when this one would work better.

You could file Trends under "most underappreciated element," but the problem is not with the element itself. The problem is that people are being given a too-narrow view of it and too little training in how to use it. It's not as obvious as some of the other elements (Quick! Guess what Patterns is about!), but there is strength in that subtlety. Yes, it's more nuanced than the other elements, and yes, you may use it less frequently, but like a valuable spice in your cupboard, just because you don't use it as often as the salt doesn't mean you don't want it.

Inherent in the idea of Trends is competition. Something has to replace something else or be in competition with something else (print books vs. e-books, gasoline-powered cars vs. electric cars, for example).

Trends is this: The direction something/someone is moving and the factors (cause/effect) influencing that change.

Trends is not this: Useless, change by itself, or bound by time.

Trends on Trial

Let's look at the arguments against Trends and then why those arguments are all wrong.

First argument: Trends is too limited.

When people defend Trends, they always draw examples from social studies. What Trends led to the Renaissance? What Trends existed in the 1960s? How have trends in eating habits changed? Yes, Trends is useful in that context, but that's a pretty narrow context. Part of the strength of Depth and Complexity is that it's useful in all content areas. Trends isn't as widely applicable as the other elements. When we try to use Trends in other content areas, it duplicates Change over Time.

Why that's all wrong:

Trends is obvious in social studies because anything with an era or -*ism* is Trends. Think Westward Expansion, the Age of Exploration, the Progressive Movement, the Bantu Migration, etc. There's your social studies, and that's where most people stop. But it's not the fault of Trends that people stop there. They're making a similar mistake to that which is made in Unanswered Questions when people ask, "What do you still want to know?"

Virtually all labs in science will use Trends. What is causing this reaction? Is the substance trending toward more or less dissolution? Why is this exothermic?

In math, we will look at Trends when we plot coordinate points, when we look at sin/cosin waves, when we look at the way denominators grow or shrink as we multiply or divide fractions. In language arts, we have Trends in the conflict of the story and in the development of the characters. In what way(s) is this character's behavior aligned with the Trends of the behavior of the other characters? In what way(s) is it not? Why is this character changing while others aren't?

Second Argument: Trends is just a special case of Over Time.

It's essentially *zoomed in* Change over Time. Any Trend is really something changing over a short period of time, so why would we add an 11th thinking tool when we already have one that does that same thing and more? While some people would defend Trends saying that it incorporates factors that cause the Trend, that's a job already done well by the Content Imperative "Contribution." You can easily discuss factors by asking, "What Contributes to this Change over Time?" Is there something that Trends covers, but Change over Time just can't (no social studies examples, please)?

Why that's all wrong:

The easy defense to this is that it's far simpler to have an eleventh prompt of Depth and Complexity than to have to add in the entire set of Content Imperatives. Most teachers using Depth and Complexity don't use the Content Imperatives (which is something else they're doing all wrong), so saying they can use Contribution instead doesn't really solve the issue that we need to look at factors and influence. Yet even if that were true – let's just accept that you could use Contribution to discuss factors influencing change – it still ignores that Trends are not bound to the linear time progression that is Change over Time.

Here's a language arts example: Let's look at the Trend in the conflict in the story (including what's causing that conflict) and layer that with the development of the character. What happens to the character when there is more or less conflict? Let's compare that to this other story. Now, let's identify a Big Idea about whether there is a connection between certain types of conflict and the static/dynamic nature of a character. That's Trends, but it's not even in the broadest interpretation of Change over Time.

In math, Trends would be what we would use to look at linear growth versus exponential growth. That isn't about time: it's about calculation, so Change over Time won't work at all.

The difference between weather and climate is Trends. The science lab example would fit here, too. Even though you could argue that labs look at Change over Time, that ignores the reality of simultaneity: oftentimes in a lab, multiple things are happening at once, all of which are influencing outcome. Also, sometimes change occurs in a single moment, and using Change over Time ignores that the power often lies not in the time that passed, but in the power of the catalyst.

Third Argument: Maybe *you* love Trends, but the Depth and Complexity tools should be student tools.

Your kids should be the ones wielding them. Do they have a clear understanding of this Prompt? Do they understand how it is significantly different from Change over Time? Or is it something they pretend to understand?

Why that's all wrong:

Oh! An opportunity to use my favorite teaching quote of all time! William Wordsworth said, "What we have loved, others will love, and we will teach them how." When teachers love something valuable, they share that love with students. If the students don't have a clear understanding, that's on the teacher (although, in the teacher's defense, most have not been taught Trends well). As we deepen in our own understanding and practice, our students will see its value. Interestingly, along with Ethics, this is the element most likely to result in real difference of opinion in discussion, which is always good ("Why is this Trend dangerous/good/bad/scary? Who hates this Trend? Who benefits? Who suffers?"). When used well, students tend to love it.

Fourth Argument: Fewer is better.

This is important because eleven of something is too many if we can cover the same ideas with ten. And if we could cover the same ground in 8, that would be even better (but that's another post!). And don't even get us started on those "new prompts" of Depth and Complexity.

Why that's all wrong:

It's not wrong, exactly. Yes, fewer is better, but only if we don't need the things we're eliminating. We need Trends because it does have unique applications. The answer is not to get rid of Trends; the answer is to use Trends better.

What Are Some Sample Question Stems?

Low-Level (Beware!)

What are the trends in ___?

Apply

- Can you explain the causes of this Trend in a way that would make sense to someone who knew nothing about it?
- Take the Trend identified in ___ and apply it to this situation/lab/problem/character.

Analyze

- How could the same factors have resulted in a different effect?
- How is this Trend similar/different from this other Trend?

Evaluate

- In what ways did the strength/weakness of ___ necessitate ___?
- Which of the factors influencing ___ is likely to be the longest/shortest lasting?
- In what ways were the effects disproportionate to the cause(s)?
- How important is this Trend?
- Who cares most/least about this Trend?
- In what ways is this Trend misunderstood?

- What influence will this Trend have in the next chapter/problem/step?
- If you could trace this outcome to a single event, what would it be? Is it possible or desirable to try to do so?
- What is the best first step in this problem?

Synthesize

- Is it valid to say that without x, y wouldn't have happened?
- Predict what would happen if x factor were removed from the equation/situation.
- How could a minor change have resulted in a very different outcome?
- Which factor could be most easily adjusted that would result in the greatest change?
- Who would be most confused by this Trend?
- What could halt this Trend? Would it be worth it?
- What happens if you choose the wrong first step in this problem?

What Are Some Sample Uses?

Trends are always complex, so resist the urge to oversimply this element with activities that ask *only* for identification of Trends.

We've already explained that Trends looks at the forces acting on something to create the trend, and it also looks at the impact of the trend. You can begin with having students notice a trend (for example, urbanization). Then, they analyze the cause of that trend (Why *do* people move to cities?). They can look at whether the reasons are the same as they have been in the past. Then, they can analyze the effects of this. How does urbanization affect the environment? The voting power of rural residents? The availability of locally sourced food?

Trends looks at the difference between change and stasis, so asking students to identify or analyze that difference can lead to interesting discussion. For example, the planets in our solar systems are in predictable, static orbits, but the universe itself is constantly expanding. How do the competing trends of expansion and fixed orbit influence our understanding of space?

Have students look for gaps and relationships. Do elements or groups move closer to or farther away from each other?

Students should examine relationships among trends. If elements on the Periodic Table are trending toward greater electron affinity and ionization energy as they are place more in the upper right of the Table, is there a connection between those trends?

In a language arts class, you may ask students to look at a period piece through this lens. In the novel *Esperanza Rising*, students may be given a task such as, "Evaluate the political, social, and economic factors that influenced Esperanza's journey. Which had the greatest impact on her and her family? Which had the least? Which affect you?

We hate to give a social studies example because they tend to be so common, yet Trends is essential there. Ask students to analyze how trends led to change in government (for instance, changes in Spanish rule led to the Texas Revolution).

Trends is a powerful lens for self-reflection as well. Are my grades/work/effort trending upward or downward? Do I notice trends in how I approach work depending upon the type of work or whom I'm working with? Lisa uses it in a Reflection she has students create for themselves where they choose a representative sample of grades, look at their strengths and opportunities, how they've changed over the course of the year, and then the trends in their achievement.

Reflection

S U Z Y   S T U D E N T

Sample Assignments

Color Lab	87
Lab report average	84
Daily Quiz Average	91
Presentation	82

Strengths/Opps

STRENGTHS: I understand the material well. I enjoy taking the quizzes. I can follow the scientific method in a lab in class.

OPPORTUNITIES: When I wait until the last minute, I have trouble creating it in the way I see in my mind. I need to check for small errors more carefully.

Changes

At the beginning of the year, I was nervous about the quizzes. Now, I'm more confident. I'm not as worried about the Bs.

Trends

My grades are trending slightly upward, although the rate has slowed. My knowledge is trending more steeply upward.

Interesting things result when you ask students to evaluate a trend, knowing they'll find stasis. This happens if you ask questions like, "How can you describe the trend in the amount of water on the Earth?" Because the water cycle is a closed system, the amount remains the same, but students want to find something (usually) and often end up drawing narrow distinctions (such as trends in fresh, flowing versus salty, frozen water). Trends can be leveraged to create curiosity.

Climate change is Trends, even though it sounds like Change over Time. Don't get upset with Trends over this confusion because it happens with Patterns and Rules, too. Why is it Trend, not Change over Time? Because the key is not the passage of time, but rather the cause/effect. Climate change is more of a cycle than the linear Change over Time allows. Students could investigate which is more vulnerable to climate change, producers or consumers?

One of the key thinking skills associated with Trends is prioritizing, so consider if you could have students prioritize the response to Trends. To pick up the self-reflection piece again, we could have a student identify not on the Trends in their work, but also the best reaction to that Trend.

How Do I Introduce It to Students?

Let's accept going in that Trends is often misunderstood. Part of the problem is that it's introduced incorrectly because the people introducing it don't understand it, either. Hopefully, our little debate above has helped you move toward an understanding of Trends that will fix that for you and your students. Here's how to do that.

Show pictures of old trends in fashion. The 70's and 80's are great for awkward trends, and so is technology. It's important to show that the trends wax and wane. For instance, cell phones started out huge (remember car phones that took up the whole trunk?) and then got small and then are getting bigger again (phablets). Help students understand some of the forces that influence trends (media, developing technology, etc.).

Explain that when you're using the Trends element, you're looking at direction – not just that something *is* changing or in what way it's different, but the directionality of that change. You're also looking at what caused that change.

A quick read of a book like those in the *If You Give a Mouse a Cookie* series can be effective in teaching the idea of cause and effect – because this happened, then this happened. This works even with older students to help them understand that with Trends, we're looking at the why.

Be sure to introduce Trends when you have content that matches it. This element benefits particularly well from an introduction followed quickly by application.

10

ETHICS

ETHICS MUST LURE STUDENTS into considering the pros and cons of a topic. It's our favorite, go-to element because it so quickly invigorates any discussion. You want to get students fired up? Just ask, "Is it fair...?"

Ethics: What It Must Do

Ethics forces students to question their opinions. Ethics must involve the taking of a position. This prompt draws students' attention to the good and bad within a topic. It should spark opportunities for debate and chances to think from other points of view. It must allow for open discussion and must lead to deep thinking. If it's shallow, it's not Ethics.

Ethics: This, Not That

Too many teachers trying to use Ethics get caught up in the term "ethics" and think that the thing being discussed has to be an ethical issue. They then think, "Oh, this element isn't for me because how many ethical issues are in *addition*?" That's the wrong way to look at it.

To use Ethics, you'll need to understand that not all Ethics issues are controversial in the common sense of the word. When we look at pros and cons, it's not necessarily a source of disagreement, yet that's Ethics. When we discuss the choices of a character, that's not political, yet it's Ethics. When we look at different ways to solve a problem, that's not going to end up in the news, but it's Ethics.

We might ask students to evaluate the pros and cons of a certain kind of organizational structure or set up of a lab. These aren't controversial ideas, yet they're Ethics.

That said, Ethics sometimes is controversial, and because of that, you'll need to do a few other things well to prepare students for that kind of discourse.

You'll need an emotionally safe classroom because Ethics gets tricky, and students have to have a clear understanding of how to disagree appropriately. Be prepared to explicitly teach students:

- How to disagree appropriately
- How to listen respectfully even if someone is saying something you disagree with
- Just because someone sees something differently from you does not make them a bad person

Another mistake teachers make is to inject themselves into the discussion. You need to be willing to stay neutral yourself. This is hard sometimes, but it's necessary. Teachers are in a position of power and authority in a classroom, so if they weigh in on the issue at hand, it often shuts down discussion or makes students see their teacher as their opponent. That's not the dynamic we're going for. Feel free to be a provocateur, pushing back against weak thinking, but keep your opinions to yourself to ensure full and robust discussion.

You'll also need something worth discussing. Any discussion about a flat secondary character is unlikely to lead anywhere interesting. Use Ethics for situations where you can see your students have multiple opinions. Now, sometimes they may not realize they have differing opinions, but the right questions ("What if we/you/it did this...") can lead them to a more invigorated mindset.

When You'll Struggle:

You'll struggle with Ethics if you're not willing for there to be a little controversy or disagreement, so if even gentle conflict stresses you out, you'll have a hard time.

You'll also struggle with Ethics if you're too comfortable with conflict because you may not manage the classroom in a way that invites discussion, not argument. They're different, and Ethics needs discussion, not fighting.

You'll struggle with Ethics if you don't see the ethical issues available in your content. Sometimes teachers think all Ethics issues are political questions, and that narrow view is not going to move you forward with this element. For example, these are possible Ethics issues:

- Should a character have chosen a different path?
- Why do we begin the problem with this set up, as opposed to a different one?
- Should geographical place names be changed to reflect more contemporary views?
- What should happen when someone violates the rules of lab safety?
- The test key said the answer was this. Make the argument that there is actually a better choice.

For example, in an 8th grade standard, students are expected to "explain how Spanish greed for riches led to their need for a cheap and dependable labor force in the New World." Push back against that with a question like, "'Greed' is a strong, negative term. Is it fair to call the Spaniards greedy when everyone wanted the same thing?"

You'll also struggle if you keep Ethics too serious. Allow it to be a little playful. Asking questions like, "Is it fair for the Earth to always be the third planet from the Sun? Should we take turns?" allows students to have a little fun with content while also deeply considering implications.

What are Some Sample Question Stems?

Low-Level (Beware!)

What are the ethics in ____?

Apply

- What are the problems we encounter when we ____?
- What controversies do we see? Which is most divisive?
- What biases/prejudices do you see?
- Do you know of another instance when this same issue resulted in a different outcome? Was that outcome more or less fair?
- Separate out fact from opinion in this argument.

Analyze

- In this complex issue, how can we find the core ethical question?
- What assumptions does ___ need you to accept in order to agree that ___?

Evaluate

- In what ways was/is _____ cheating?
- Rank the problems associated with _____ in order from most to least difficult to solve/important/etc.
- Would it be ethical to _____ and why/why not?

- Justify why it would/would not be fair to _____.
- In what way are the claims that _____ valid? In what way are they not?
- Is this con a strong enough reason to make this change?
- Which of the ethical dilemmas is least likely to be solved and why?
- How would you have handled _____?
- If there are so many cons, why is _____ still in play/up for discussion?
- Why doesn't everyone think about ___ the way that ___ does?
- Is it fair to say that _____ means ___?
- Which three Details best support the claim that ___?

Synthesize

- If the people had followed the rules, how would it have ended differently?
- What are the pros and cons to _____ from the perspective of ___?
- Describe how much change there would be if _____ happened? Would that change be ultimately positive or negative?
- Would this have been more/less ethical in the past/future?
- Which of the ethical dilemmas faced by _____ causes the most struggle?

- How would x character have solved the ethical issue faced by y character?

- What changes could we make to make this thing more fair/just/right?

- Condense this ethical argument into a sentence of no more than six words.

- What could have happened next if this other choice had been made?

What are Some Sample Uses?

Like all of the elements, infusing Ethics is primarily a matter of questioning. Remember, these are thinking skills, not worksheet skills. You can apply Ethics across nearly any content area for an instant boost in depth. What ethical issues does a character face... or cause? What ethical problems happened because of an event in history? Or what problems led to an event? What are the issues with the periodic table? Or with a specific element on the periodic table? Is it fair to interfere with the water cycle by building dams, even though they often provide a clean energy source?

Which ethical issues did George Washington handle most successfully? Or more poorly? Is it fair for one person to be the king or queen for life? Is it fair to judge people in the past according to current social norms? What are the pros and cons of using a calculator instead of computation? Why would guessing and checking be better than setting up a proportion to solve this problem? Which would be quicker? Which would be more likely to be correct?

You can apply Ethics to questions of fairness or justice. Even a question that seems silly can lead to some interesting discussions: Is a food web fair? Which form of natural disaster is least fair? Is it fair that poetry doesn't have to follow the rules of prose? Is it fair that some animals are so much bigger than other animals?

In math, I use the Ethics tool to draw students' attention to common errors, dangerous shortcuts, or confusing aspects of a topic. You can also use Ethics to create deeper meaning in solving math problems. For example, we've seen a teacher who took a story problem that asked how many people Ms. Smith should invite to her party if she has ninety-five tacos and wants to make sure everyone has six, and ask students, "What should Ms. Smith do if some people want more than six tacos, but there aren't enough for everyone to have more than six?"

We've also seen the plotting of coordinate points on a line that use the grid as a road and a taxi trip as the way to ask students to compute the distance from one set of coordinate points to another, and then asked, "Would it be fair for the taxi driver to charge $10 for the fare?"

As mentioned earlier, you can use Ethics to challenge the content itself. Why should/should not monogons and/or digons be recognized as polygons?

Seriously, we could play with Ethics all day.

How Do I Introduce It to Students?

Ethics is super fun to introduce to students with the "Okay/Not Okay" Game. Come up with a list of questions that address simple ethical issues, like:

- Is it okay or not okay to not fully stop at a stop sign if you're out in the middle of nowhere?

- Is it okay or not okay to give your friend the sandwich you didn't like out of your lunchbox and not tell your dad when he asks you if you liked the sandwich he made you?

- Is it okay or not okay to look at someone's paper during a test if you're just checking your answers, not cheating?

- Is it okay or not okay to tell someone their new shirt looks good when you really don't like it, but you don't want to hurt their feelings?

- Is it okay to talk about people behind their backs if you only say nice things about them?

- Is it okay or not okay to keep money that you find on the floor of the grocery store?

- Is it okay or not okay to use your neighbor's unsecured wifi?

Choose situations your students will be familiar with, and the more likely there is to be disagreement, the better. Take one of the questions that seems to spark a lot of discussion, and dive deeper into it with a pros/cons T-chart. What are the pros of using your neighbor's unsecured wifi? What are the cons/risks?

Explain that the Ethics element looks at what is fair, the pros and cons of something, and what is right.

It helps us look at a story like *Goldilocks and the Three Little Bears* and say, "Was she a traveler in need or a burglar?" or "Were the Colonists patriots or traitors?" We use it to look at our own actions, such as if it's okay to copy someone's homework, and we use it to look at the pros and cons of what we're studying, such as what are the pros or cons of choosing a certain organizational structure.

11

CHANGE OVER TIME

WITH CHANGE OVER TIME, we move from the "depth" prompts to our first example of "complexity." Rather than diving more deeply into a single topic, we're going to go broader - connecting with other ideas.

Change over Time: What it Must Do

Change over Time focuses students on how an idea, topic, person, or event has changed over time. It must evaluate the change, deciding if the change was positive or negative, necessary or unnecessary, what are its benefits and drawbacks?

Change over Time: This, Not That

If you're only looking at Change over Time in a narrow sense of something that was one way and is now a different way, you're leaving a lot of thinking power on the table. To fully take advantage of the power of this element, you've got to really get into the weeds. Unlike Big Idea that takes a 10,000-foot view, Change over Time combines the big, overarching idea of a change that occurred and marries it to a close examination of the effects of the change.

This: What was the significance of the change?
Not This: What changed?

This: In what ways would Mendeleev approve of the changes to the Periodic Table? Which changes would he like least?
Not (Only) This: How did the Periodic Table of the Elements change over time?

This: Who was most affected by the way so-and-so changed through the course of the story and why?
Not This: Did so-and-so change through the course of the story?

This: Which way of solving proportion problems makes more sense to you, the old way of cross-multiplying, or finding a ratio? Which way is faster? Which way will help you most in the future?
Not (Only) This: What was the old way of solving proportion problems?

These examples may seem laughably simplistic, yet we see these types of mistakes all of the time. Sometimes, the jump from low-level questioning to high-level questioning is only a few words, yet it's leaps and bounds up Bloom's pyramid.

When you're working with Change over Time, you're looking at all of the implications of that change, as well as predictions about what might change in the future.

What are Some Sample Question Stems?

Low-Level (Beware!)

- What has changed over time?

Apply

- How would your teacher last year have discussed this?
- Can you predict when you might use this again in your future?
- How can you tell there was a change?
- Who/what was most impacted by the change?

Analyze

- What forces do you think are acting on ____ to force change? To maintain stasis?
- How are these ideas related across the past, present, and future?
- How are these ideas related within or during a particular period of time?
- How has time affected the accuracy/relevance of the information?

- Why is ____ changing? Why is ____ not changing?
- What prompted the need for this change?
- Is ____ changing faster than ____ was before?
- Can you predict what the next change might be? When it might be?
- Will ____ continue to change at the same rate of speed?
- Analyze the motive for the change. Were the motives all aligned?

Evaluate

- What are the pros and cons of this change (or lack of change)?
- Do you think this will become more or less important to you over time?
- How different do you think this is from when your parents learned it?
- Which is better: the way ____ was in the past, the way ____ is now, or how ____ will be in the future?
- How much of this change is fact and how much is opinion?
- Make the argument that this change was inevitable.
- Make the argument that this change was preventable.
- How effective was ____ in explaining the need for the change?
- What further changes would you recommend?
- Which change was most important/moral/valid/logical/appropriate/popular/etc.?

Synthesize

- How would this story have been different if it had taken place during a different time period?
- How much would it have changed if we stopped later/earlier?
- Would the impact have been greater or less if we had stretched out the change over a longer period of time?
- Would the impact have been greater or less if we had condensed the change to a shorter period of time?
- In what ways could the change be undone?

What are Some Sample Uses?

If you've gotten this far, it won't shock you that this element is all about asking good questions that get kids thinking. As with the other elements, use the Possible Products list in the Appendix for ways students can answer these questions.

Change over Time naturally works well in a study of literature. How do we see a character changing throughout a story? How does an author change? Or how does literature itself change over time?

Students can be asked to trace the changes in a character over the course of the story and identify ways in which the character changes and ways in which he/she stays the same and then support their claim that he/she is either a static or dynamic character (Big Idea).

In math, questions that require uniform rate tables to solve are Change over Time. Consider a question like this, "A 555-mile, 5-hour plane trip was flown at two speeds. For the first part of the trip, the average speed was 105 mph. Then the tailwind picked up, and the remainder of the trip was flown at an average speed of 115 mph. For how long did the plane fly at each speed?"

The student sets up a uniform rate table, and the teacher would ask, "What happens over time to the plane? Would it be fair to charge passengers more for planes that fly faster?" (See that combination with Ethics?) You could then add an extra level of challenge by asking, "What would your hourly pay rate have to be to justify paying an extra $150 for the faster rate of speed?" It's trickier than it seems.

Change over Time is perfect for examining velocity. Many, many science topics are time dependent. Consider asking students to explain the processes that led to the formation of sedimentary rocks and fossil fuels.

In social studies, we can look at the impact of Change over Time with tasks such as, "Identify and explain how changes resulting from the Industrial Revolution led to conflict among sections of the United States."

If a standard asks students to explain how Natives, Africans, and Europeans changed when they encountered one another in the New World, Change over Time will lead to tasks such as, "Write a letter to your family in Africa explaining how you have been affected by your encounter with Europeans. Be specific."

For a higher-level government course, we can combine Trends with Change over Time in a task such as, "In what ways did the weaknesses in the Articles of Confederation necessitate the drafting of the Constitution? (Trends) Of those weaknesses, pick the one you think was most likely to impact the country for the longest period of time and create a single Google slide demonstrating your reasoning using no more than 15 words and two images."

How Do I Introduce It to Students?

Ian likes to introduce change over time using photographs that, quite literally, show the effects of time:

- McDonald's menus and buildings
- TV sets, phones, computers, or other technology
- Clothing or hairstyles
- And, most popularly, photos of himself

At first, students will point out the funny surface details in the "old" photos (whether McDonald's different shaped buildings or Ian's once-long hair), and you can use this to point out that it's not just appearances that are changing, but beliefs, laws, feelings, and other less-obvious traits.

Change over Time is constantly happening, and it's a powerful idea to realize that we are currently in the middle of a change, we just don't know what's coming next yet. You can emphasize this with a beginning/middle/end organizer that is, instead, a past/present/future organizer.

- Past: TV sets were once large, heavy boxes that received channels through antenna.

- Present: TV sets have become thin and wide rectangles that receive channels through cable or satellite, but also movies and shows through the internet.

- Future: TVs will probably become even thinner with more realistic pictures and show virtual reality.

- Past: McDonalds buildings had giant arches in the building, they sold burgers for 5¢, and only offered a few items.

- Present: McDonald's buildings have brown roofs and look like little houses, they have a huge selection of items, and they have wide range of prices.

- Future: Perhaps McDonald's will need to focus on selling fewer and healthier foods.

- Past: Mr. Byrd had long hair and played guitar in a band.

- Present: Mr. Byrd works with teachers, parents, and students to improve schools. And he has much less hair!

- Future: Mr. Byrd would like to...

Another way to introduce Change over Time to students is to look at it from the lens of problems and challenges. Lisa asks students to think about problems that people used to have that we don't have anymore. Because students are young, you will need to make sure they've been exposed to some of the possibilities. Images or videos can be an effective way to do this.

Some examples her students have come up with include:

- Getting a busy signal when you call home
- Everyone wanting to watch the same show on TV
- Not being able to get ahold of someone when they're not at home to answer the phone.
- Waiting for news until the newspaper comes out the next day

She then asks them to think of things that didn't used to be a problem a long time ago, but that are problems or challenges now. Sample responses include:

- Needing to find a place to plug in your phone or device
- People messaging you and getting mad when you don't text them back right away
- Social media bullying
- Texting and driving

Then, students consider how our view of certain things has changed, again using images. They look at things such as:

- Galileo (or other well-known scientist)
- Smoking
- Families
- Butter
- Cursive writing

This helps students see that part of Change over Time is not just what has changed, but also how the thing itself can stay the same while people's attitudes change.

12

ACROSS DISCIPLINES

ACROSS DISCIPLINES ASKS HOW things are connected with each other, both within and without an area of study. How are things related? How is this learning like this other learning? It is an exciting, undervalued element.

Across Disciplines: What It Must Do

To use Across Disciplines effectively, students must be willing to forge new idea pathways. They must create thought bridges that allow them to connect their learning to prior learning and learning outside of the narrow topic being discussed. Across Disciplines forces analogy. Students have to say, "This is like that because..." even when the comparison is not obvious. It's exactly the kind of thinking our students are asked to do and that they often do not do well. This is one of the most powerful of the elements when used effectively. Unfortunately, all too often it's hardly used at all.

Across Disciplines: This, Not That

This element is underused because, like Trends, people don't understand it well enough. Too many people think that Across Disciplines is only about how something applies to science *and* social studies or language arts *and* math. Most often, they think, "Oh, Across Disciplines just means language arts and history." That's not quite right. It *is* that, but it's also much more than that.

Here's what people are missing: Across Disciplines is also about how ideas and concepts are connected within the *same* field. This is the element that lets a teacher ask, "In what way is this like the other thing we learned last week/last month/last year?"

Do you see the difference? It's not saying you must come out of your content area and jump to another one. It's saying that you can also use it to bridge the ideas across your own discipline, too. It is both intra- and inter-disciplinary.

> This: What thinking tools did you use to solve this problem that you have used in other problems as well?
>
> Not (Only) This: How is this problem like something you'd see in science?

The "Not (Only) This" example above is a great question, but it's not the *only* kind of question for Across Disciplines. Knowing this expands the use of the element exponentially. Here are a couple of other examples:

This: In what ways is this character similar to [insert character from another story or a historical figure]?

Not (Only) This: How does this story relate to economics?

This: Compare the economics of the Gold Rush to the economics of the oil boom.

And This: How do we see science, history, and economics in the Gold Rush? Which of those elements is most important to understanding the Gold Rush?

It's easy to understand why people make this mistake. Across Disciplines has a branding issue. It would be less confusing if it didn't use the word "disciplines." That makes us think that we must cross content lines to use it. Don't get hung up on the name. Just focus on the idea of connection.

Across Disciplines is one of the three elements of the framework that are identified as "complexity" elements. It asks, "How does this topic represent an intersection of ideas or fields?" If you read Chapter 1, you may remember that the complexity elements are those that ask student to "mak[e] relationships between and among ideas, connect other concepts, and layer a why/how interdisciplinary approach that connects and bridges to other disciplines." This is the element that does that.

What are Some Sample Question Stems?

Low-Level (Beware!)

- How are there different disciplines here?

- Is this used in other areas?

Apply

- What are alternative connections we could make?
- What does a [fill in discipline] think of this?
- Apply the ideas of [different experience or discipline] to this problem/topic.

Analyze

- In what ways is this the same as _____?
- Explain why you saw this differently this time than the last time you studied it.
- What are the common elements among _____?
- How is this related to _____?

Evaluate

- Judge the validity of this connection.
- Why is it important to recognize this connection?
- In what ways does this connection deepen our understanding of _____?
- What seems to be the weakest connection between these two things that is still valid?
- Which of the common elements among these topics is the strongest?
- When we talked about this before, the greatest challenge was _____. Is that still the same?

- When/where does this comparison fall apart?
- Looking at the two resources, which one is most strongly related to what we learned already?
- How were these connections easy/difficult to identify?

Synthesize

- How would a ____ (disciplinarian) interpret this evidence?
- How could we make a better connection?
- What are some questions a ____ (disciplinarian) might ask of this?
- What would a ____ (disciplinarian) think about this?
- How would you explain this idea to a [insert discipline here]?
- Create a chain of between three and seven ideas that connect these two ideas.

What are Some Sample Uses?

The question stems above will help you apply Across Disciplines in an intra-disciplinary way (within the discipline). Here are some ideas for inter-disciplinary application of the element.

Use Across Disciplines to onboard students to new content ideas by sharing connections with previously learned material, even if it was in a different class. For example, if you're looking at map projections in geography for the first time, you may want to harken back to what they've learned previously about spheres.

You could ask, "Where do we see triangles in places other than math?" [Warning: When Lisa asked this question of third graders, one responded, "My dad's in a love triangle." Ah, teacher life.]

If you're introducing shapes, ask students to create riddles involving a hexagon or maps that use a certain number of shapes or having them research the connection between polygons and honeybees or lava.

If your math students are learning about functions, you can deepen this by having them consider the ways that countries and capitals are also a one-to-one relationship. If you're talking about European exploration of the New World, you can compare it to the motives that guide space exploration now.

Use it to deepen understanding of new material very quickly. For example, a common Kindergarten standard is to help students learn that people live in houses and that houses look different in different places. Across Disciplines allows you to show pictures of several houses and ask questions such as, "Which house would a termite like least? Which house is most likely to catch fire?" We can even ask students to complete jump content by having them do a little math with the houses, counting them up or sorting them into categories.

Differentiate the thinking level for high ability students by requiring the application of the Across Disciplines lens to the subject. Consider this essay prompt: Write an essay explaining how Trends in poetry and art both reflect changing social mores of World War I-era Europe.

Use it to think more critically about content. For example, have art students analyze a painting from one of the Dutch masters through the lens of how an Impressionist would consider it.

You can save instructional time by conflating tasks. If your students are reading a poem like Shel Silverstein's *Band Aids*, they can count the bandages and make then make fractions of how many were on limbs versus the rest of the body or similar task.

Get kids who see themselves as a "math" person or a "science" person to embrace another subject by having them do something "math-y" or "science-y" with content that otherwise wouldn't be. For example, an escape room activity can be done with a social studies lesson that involves solving math problems to unlock the boxes. Students could create a rebus of the Declaration of Independence. Have students studying the water cycle create a timeline of the changing understanding of the water cycle over centuries. The possibilities for this are endless.

An added bonus? It's an opportunity to work with your colleagues in different grades or departments!

Advanced Methods

Ready to go broader? Consider this scenario: At a high school, math, PE, photography, art, and biology teachers all worked together to create a cross-disciplinary project. The photography students videotaped the PE students throwing the discus. Math students analyzed the video and calculated the angle of the thrower's arm to his/her body and correlated that angle to the distance the discus was thrown. They then identified a range of ideal angle. Biology students analyzed the video to identify the muscles and tendons that bore the greatest burden in the throwing.

The PE students then attempted to adjust the angle of their arm to their body and the coaches worked on developing the muscles that the biology students had identified. The art students drew human torsos throwing a discus, focusing on the muscles and tendons identified by the biology students (the torsos didn't have skin). The advanced students in each group worked together to create a display that was in the library called "Discus: The Art and Science of the Throw." That is next level Across Disciplines.

An English teacher worked with a French teacher to get students interested in poetry. The French students translated the poem *Study in Hands* by French poet Gautier into English. They gave their translations to an English class. The students in the English class did a comparison of the Gautier poem to an Emily Dickinson poem of their choice (Dickinson and Gautier were contemporaries). This built a bond of personal connection, not just curriculum. From then on, the students had a connection to "their" translator.

How Do I Introduce It to Students?

A fun way to introduce Across Disciplines is to show students a visual representation of the "Six Degrees of Kevin Bacon" game (just do a quick internet search – it'll come up). Then, show the meme "Six Degrees of Kevin Bacon" that has all of his dance moves identified by math angles. That one's harder to find, so we've got it available for you at giftedguild.com/dcextras.

Discuss that, while we don't naturally think of math angles when we think of dancing, math is indeed there. Explain that often in class we'll discuss the thing we're learning about, and we'll want to explore how it connects to other things that may seem completely disconnected.

Next, play the word association game. To play, a student, chosen randomly, says one word out loud. The next person (you'll have to identify the path you want students to follow) has to quickly say a word that has some connection with the previous word. And so on. You'll have to decide if you want to allow challenges, or if you're just going to go with whatever kids say (I'd do that option myself).

When you stop, point out just how far you came from the original word, and yet there were connections all along the way. Explain that in class, not only will you be making connections between entire fields of study like math and social studies, but also connections between what you learned today and what you learned last week or even last year. When we think of Across Disciplines, we're thinking about how what we're looking at is connected with other things we know and have learned. It's the Six Degrees of Kevin Bacon element. It asks us to make connections, even if they don't seem that obvious at first.

13

MULTIPLE PERSPECTIVES

MULTIPLE PERSPECTIVES IS THE ELEMENT that asks students to consider how another person or thing would think about a topic. It adds complexity by encouraging a broader view of a topic. It is perhaps the thinking skill most lacking in the world today, and we do our students a great service by helping them become strong in this ability.

Multiple Perspectives: What It Must Do

When we're explaining Multiple Perspectives to students, we need to make sure they understand that perspective is often dependent upon time, place, and culture. The exact same event can be very different when it takes place at one time over another. Even wonderful events can be much less wonderful if they're done at the wrong/inappropriate time. Students also need to understand that it's affected by our roles and responsibilities. If I'm a parent, I have a very different view of my child's staying up late than my child does. Perspective affects our interpretation of events, actions, and even facts.

Multiple Perspectives is the spatial reasoning element. You know those tasks that ask students to pick up a shape off the page, spin it around, lay it back down and recognize what it looks like now? That's Multiple Perspectives.

Without Multiple Perspectives, students' Big Ideas will be weaker, so make sure you use this element with wild abandon.

Multiple Perspectives: This, Not That

If you're using Multiple Perspectives only to examine the perspective of people (or characters), you're leaving a cool technique on the table. Teachers are usually really good at implementing Multiple Perspectives. Its straightforward nature and the alignment between what it's called and what it does seems to make for solid use. There is one little tweak we think needs to be made, though.

If you really want to use Multiple Perspectives to its fullest, you need to include the perspective of inanimate objects. Describe the rules of baseball from the perspective of the ball. Describe the experience of recess from the perspective of the playground. Describe the rotation of the Earth from the perspective of the Sun. You get the picture.

This: How does the right angle feel about the hypotenuse?
Not (Only) This: How does a mathematician feel about triangles compared to a carpenter?

This: Because of gravity, does having a greater mass mean that some planets are bossier than other planets?

Not (Only) This: Who thinks space exploration is more valuable, astronauts or science fiction fans?

This: Would this be more valuable to the numerator or the denominator?

Not (Only) This: Who would use this more often, a mathematician or an engineer?

This: Does the cover of this book think it represents the story well?

Not (Only) This: Do you think the cover of this book represents the story well?

In addition to incorporating inanimate objects, it's also important to combine this element with other elements. For example, you need to look at the pros and cons of the perspectives, rather than just list the perspectives. That requires Ethics. You need to look at the factors influencing the perspectives, and that's Trends. Multiple Perspectives is a social creature. It needs to combine to come alive.

What are Some Sample Question Stems?

Low-Level (Beware!)

- What are some different perspectives about this?
- Who thinks differently?

Apply

- Can you explain why _____ felt _____?
- What are other possible perspectives that were not discussed or considered?
- What biases are at work here? Which one is most influential?
- How would you use this in ____?

Analyze

- Describe how we can hold two opposing views on this subject simultaneously.
- Are we looking at this more from the perspective of strength or weakness?
- Compare the way that _____ sees _____ versus the way _____ sees it.
- How were the motivations of _____ and _____ different from each other?
- Who might see this differently?
- Is this more important to _____ or ____?

Evaluate

- How has the way you see this changed? Do you expect it to change again?
- Which perspective is hardest to defend?
- Whose perspective do most people agree with and why?

Synthesize

- Who wants ____ to happen the most? Who wants it to happen least?
- Why would a test writer think this was worth creating a test question for?
- How differently do you think you feel about this than your teacher does?
- Defend the perspective that is least like your own.
- If ____ had happened, how might the perspective have changed?
- Why would ____ interpret this data differently from ____?
- How would the story have been different if it had been told from the point of view of ____?
- Would ____ think it was fair to say ____? Would ____ agree?

What are Some Sample Uses?

Point of view is literally one of the literary elements, so we will clearly be using Multiple Perspectives frequently in language arts. Students might analyze the conflict in a story from various characters' points of view. They might consider how different people might interpret a story's moral or how a character from another story would have seen the conflict. They might use textual evidence to defend the point of view of a character.

Historical events take on new complexity when we think about them through the lens of Multiple Perspectives. What was the

American Revolution like from John Adams' perspective compared to that of an ordinary colonist? What about someone living in France? How did different groups of people interpret the events of the Boston Tea Party?

Math students can look at problems through the viewpoints of different components (the operators, the numbers themselves, variables, etc.). Who is more powerful in the problem, the operator or the number?

A biome takes on new meanings when we think from multiple perspectives. How is the importance of the rain forest different when viewed from the perspective of a medical company compared to a local logger or a real estate firm? View the water cycle from the perspectives of a water droplet and groundwater. View the food web from the perspectives of a producer and consumer.

Students can compare and contrast two different points of view on a problem. For example, how do architects and clients see projects differently? Who is more worried about cost? Time? The overall success of the project? Who is most harmed when it goes badly?

How Do I introduce It to Students?

School is a perfect topic for introducing multiple perspective. A student may see school in one way, but a teacher, principal or custodian will see the same school quite differently. A hamburger takes on an entirely different perspective when viewed from the perspective of a vegetarian, a chef, a rancher, or a Hindu.

For a more thorough introduction, you can show photos of the same place taken from different perspectives and ask questions about them. I use photos of bodies of water (under, over, sideways) and buildings (from the ground, from the sky, from weird angles). Ask questions such as:

- Where would you have to position yourself to be able to take that photograph?
- Who would most need that photograph?
- Who would have this perspective?
- Who would benefit most from this perspective?

Then show an image of chalk art taken from the angle it was supposed to be seen and then the opposite angle. (You can find the one Lisa uses at giftedguild.com/dcextras.) Explain that sometimes, perspective is everything.

Show the picture of the different people all examining an elephant (find it at giftedguild.com/dcextras). They all think the elephant is something different because they only see what they see (It's a wall! It's a tree! It's a fan!). Explain that our perspective can narrow our view to the point that we don't fully or accurately understand what we're looking at.

PART III:

CONTENT IMPERATIVES

14

THE CONTENT IMPERATIVES

I BOUGHT A NICE LAPTOP, thinking, "I will never need a more powerful tool than this." Of course, one day my needs outgrew that laptop and I bought another, even more powerful laptop.

The eleven Depth and Complexity prompts may seem like more power than your students could ever handle. But if you work with upper-elementary, middle school, or high school students who have five to ten years of Depth and Complexity experience, you'll realize that you do, indeed, need a more powerful laptop.

Enter: The Content Imperatives

The Content Imperatives are an additional set of five thinking tools that augment Depth and Complexity. They're an add-on or an expansion pack. They build on what you already have. The five tools are:

- Origin: focuses on the beginning of an idea.

- Contribution: focuses on how one factor affects (or contributes to) an idea.
- Convergence: focuses on the effect of multiple factors coming together.
- Parallel: how one idea can be similar to another.
- Paradox: how an idea can be pulled in two opposite directions.

In the same way a *Settlers of Catan* expansion pack allows more players to participate, the Content imperatives allow more ideas to be generated. They are a strong lever to lift thinking, and they're a great way for teachers who are becoming stronger in their DC practice to move to next level play.

Combine with the Elements

The biggest mistake we see people make with the Content Imperatives is to consider them as just five more icons. The *true power* of the Content Imperatives comes from combining them with Depth and Complexity. They aren't just five more tools; they are five tools that enhance the power of Depth and Complexity. They allow for more precision, as well as depth and breadth, of thinking.

Look at how the Content Imperatives push the Ethics prompt into new territory.

- Identify the Origin of this Ethical issue.

- Decide which factors Contributed the most to make this Ethical problem better or worse.
- What unexpected factors Converged to solve the Ethical problem?
- How could a Parallel Ethical problem shed light on this problem?
- In what ways was this Ethical issue a Paradox, leading to positive and negative outcomes?

The Content Imperatives keep us on one prompt of Depth and Complexity for much longer than if we had just used that Ethics prompt on its own. It pushes students even deeper into your content.

Now, we don't think kids' heads will implode or anything if you use a Content Imperative without a tool of Depth and Complexity. It's fine to ask students to "Explain the Origin of the Constitution." But, if you really want to get students thinking, use a combination like "Explain how the Convergence of Multiple Perspectives led to the US Constitution's success." Much more powerful.

Think of it in the same way as using the bottom of Bloom's with a Depth and Complexity prompt. You *could* ask "What are the Rules ...", but ideally you'll be moving towards a higher-order thinking skill. Likewise, you might use a Content Imperative in isolation, but it should be an exception. Typically, Content Imperatives are meant to be combined with Depth and Complexity, but don't worry, there aren't any Depth and

Complexity enforcers who will pull your Depth and Complexity card if you use them in isolation.

Building a Sequence of Questions

We have to be careful not to stay at the bottom of Bloom's for too long when questioning, but it can be overwhelming to jump straight to higher order thinking when we're using with Depth and Complexity elements and Content Imperatives. This is why developing a scaffolded sequence of questions is essential. We can start simple and grow to a complex level of thinking that won't discourage students. Onboard, onboard, onboard.

Here's an example:

I start with my most-complex, highest-order prompt: "Pick another example of a rebellion from history or fiction. Compare the convergence of ethical issues from that conflict with those leading to the American Revolution. How would you rank the parallel between the two conflicts on a scale of 1 (totally different) to 5 (complete parallels)?"

Now, obviously, that's a lot to break down. Start there with an eleven-year-old and you won't have a lot of success. So, instead, we can build to that prompt with simpler questions.

1. Identify three to five ethical problems that contributed to the American Revolution.
2. Describe the origin of each of these problems.
3. Explain how these ethical problems did not happen in isolation but converged to lead to the Revolution.

4. Pick another example of a rebellion from history or fiction. Identify three to five ethical problems that contributed to that conflict.

5. Compare the convergence of those problems with the convergence that lead to the American Revolution. How similar is the parallel on a scale of 1 to 5?

What was at first an overwhelmingly complex task has become a ladder that many more students can climb successfully, step by step. But not everyone needs to get all the way through step five. The grade-level expectation is probably complete at the second or third question. The opportunity to go much deeper exists for all students, however. This is what is meant by keeping a high ceiling. It doesn't mean that even your best thinkers don't also need a floor to stand on.

Introduce with Simple Content

In your scope and sequence, the Content Imperatives shouldn't be introduced until students have a solid foundation with Depth and Complexity. If you're at a school using the Framework, this may mean they aren't unveiled until 4th or 5th grade. In your own class, you might reveal them in the second trimester. Definitely don't dump five more thinking tools on students who are still finding their feet with the original eleven.

Introduce them slowly, one Imperative at a time. Five seems so manageable after eleven, but it's still five. If you go too quickly, you are likely to be going too shallowly (Yes, that's a word. We looked it up.). You want the students to feel comfortable with these new thinking tools, not overwhelmed. The same is true for you as a teacher. There is no arbitrary timeline for introducing the Content Imperatives, so don't feel rushed.

As with the Depth and Complexity prompts, it's best to introduce the Content Imperatives with content that students are already experts in. Ian's mentor teacher used a hamburger as her introductory topic. You might pick cell phones, bicycles, or a popular movie.

Be aware that when you add a Content Imperative it will push even well-known content to a point that requires some research. Students may be able to come up with "Rules about Hamburgers" off the top of their heads, but when we ask for the "Origin of a Rule about Hamburgers," we're going to need to gather some resources.

The following chapters take a closer look at each of the Content Imperatives, complete with ideas for introducing them to students.

15

CONTRIBUTION

CONTRIBUTION SEEMS LIKE such a positive Content Imperative. I mean, what could be more friendly than to recognize contribution? Yet, Contribution is also an examination of the problematic contributions as well.

Contribution: What it Must Do

Whether we're discussing art, an important event, or a mathematical expression, there are always multiple factors affecting the topic. Contribution asks students to focus on those factors.

This Content Imperative looks at the contribution, but also analyzes its value. How important is it? What was the effect of the contribution? It's a great tool for helping students develop the skill of evaluating relevance. Yes, this thing or person contributed, but to what extent was that contribution meaningful? Did it really move the needle?

Contribution: This, Not That

We've already mentioned it, but the tendency is to see contribution as purely positive. That's lovely, but it's incomplete. We have to help students understand that sometimes contribution is neutral or even negative.

Additionally, sometimes a contribution is smaller than it seems. Sometimes someone believes that their contribution was more impactful than it really was. You can think you're playing a part, but you may have a supporting role or even just a walk-on part that doesn't earn a mention in the credits. Those supporting roles are important to analyze, too, so don't leave them out.

This: In what way did _____ delay the solving of the problem?
Not (Only) This: In what way did ____ contribute to solving the problem?

This: How was the contribution of ___ less important than he/she thought it was?
Not (Only) This: How did ____ contribute to ___?

Sample Question Stems

Apply

- How does an author's specific use of language contribute to the tone of this poem?
- How would one's perspective contribute to deciding which fuel source to choose?

Analyze

- How does the passage of time contribute to weathering differently from erosion?

- Which rule contributes most to the identify of a shape: its side lengths, angle sizes, or number of parallel sides?

- Which details contribute most to an equation, the numbers, variables, or operators?

- How do consumers, producers, and decomposers each uniquely contribute to their ecosystem?

- How did a mentor contribute to this person/character's ethical choices?

- How did an event contribute to this person/character's perspective?

- Which small detail contributes most to conflict between ____ and ____?

- Who could/should have contributed, but didn't? What was the effect of that?

Evaluate

- Which ethical issue contributed the most to this character's decision?

- Which one person contributed the most to the rules formed at the Constitutional Convention?

- Which segment of the electromagnetic spectrum contributes most to the development of human civilization? Which could we do without?

How to Introduce it to Students

We're sharing two ways to introduce Contribution, one for older students and one for younger students.

With younger children, read or tell the story of *Stone Soup*. This story demonstrates the value of everyone's contribution, even if by itself it didn't seem that important. Discuss the impact that everyone's contribution made. Ask what would have happened if someone had put a tire in the soup? A bunch of dirt? Explain that sometimes contributions are unwelcome or unhelpful.

Ask them to share ways they help at home. Ask them to share ways they help at school. If you use a classroom helper system, point that out. Discuss the ways that various people at the school contribute to making the school run, from the janitor to the workers in the cafeteria to the teachers and administration. Explain that you will be using Contribution to think about these kinds of things. When they see the icon for it, they should know that they're looking at how something is helping or not helping.

With older students, show a short clip from the movie *The Emperor's Club*. The clip is near the very beginning of the movie, and it shows a teacher, played by Kevin Kline, explaining the importance of contribution. He says, "Great ambition and conquest without contribution is without significance." He then asks, "What will your contribution be? How will history remember you?"

After you show the clip, have students sketch out a Venn Diagram. Have them label the sides "home" and "school." Next, ask them to consider ways in which they contribute at home, at school, and in both home and school. They should think of things that are seen and unseen, positive and negative, small and larger.

Below the Venn diagram, have them sketch out the icon you're using for Unanswered Questions. Ask them to identify one way that they could contribute in a positive way that they are not now currently contributing at home and one way at school and what the impact of that contribution might be. If they *did* contribute in those ways, what would happen?

Show students the quote, "No snowflake in an avalanche ever feels responsible." Ask them to turn to a shoulder partner and figure out what this quote means. Discuss it as a class, making sure they arrive at the idea that when we're in a big group, we often don't realize the impact of our role. Ask them to think of real-life examples of "snowflakes" lead to "avalanches." They will often come up with things like the environment, traffic jams, and other similar ideas.

Explain that you will be using the Contribution Content Imperative to look at the ways things and people impact other things and people, positively and negatively, big and small.

16

CONVERGENCE

THINK OF PARENTS ARRIVING for Open House one at a time, spaced out evenly every three minutes. Lots of greetings, but it's somehow manageable. Now think of the reality of Open House: twenty parents walking in at the same moment. This represents a Convergence. A coming-together of multiple things all at once. When things Converge, it's quite different from when they happen sequentially. A Convergence is different than the sum of its parts.

Convergence: This, Not That

First, we need to make sure that we clearly separate Contribution and Convergence. Convergence isn't just the plural of Contribution. It's highlighting the interplay between multiple factors coming together at the same time. This interaction often leads to results that are greater than the sum of its parts. It's synergistic.

Beware asking over and over "What came together in [Situation X]?". We want to go beyond just noting that there was a convergence and instead ask about the effects of the convergence. We could ask what would happen if different elements had converged. What if we lost one of the converging elements?

> This: "Which voice was *least* important in the convergence of perspectives?"

> Or This: "What would have happened had Ben Franklin not been one of the voices?"

> Or This: "What if Abe Lincoln had been present? How would this have changed the convergence of voices?"

> Not (Just) This "How did different people converge at the Continental Congress?"

Convergence may be combined with multiple prompts of Depth and Complexity to see how the prompts themselves interact (what happens when rules, ethics, and multiple perspectives converge?).

What are Some Sample Question Stems?

Apply

- How did the convergence of perspectives shape the US Constitution?

- How do the rules followed by consumers, producers, and decomposers converge to impact their ecosystem?
- Explain how each civilization/colony/tribe/etc. was a unique convergence of technology, geography, and beliefs.
- Describe this word problem as a convergence of essential information, neutral information, and distracting information.

Analyze

- Compare the convergence of details that leads to erosion with the convergence that leads to weathering.
- How do language, rules, and patterns converge to make this author's voice unique? Contrast this author's convergence with another author.

Evaluate

- How did the author use a convergence of setting, plot, character, and language to establish their message? Was this convergence balanced or did one part do more work?
- Shapes are defined by a convergence of rules. Which shape's convergence is most unique?

Synthesize

- Think about how a character's rules, ethics, and language converge to form their perspective. Express that perspective as a single big idea.

When asking students to explore a convergence, it is always best to make sure they understand the contribution of each factor on its own before looking at the convergence of those factors.

What are Some Sample Activities?

Take any situation with multiple factors and tease them apart. Examine them individually and then look at how they come together to do something new.

In science, an earthquake, tornado, fire, mountain, or explosion are all the result of a convergence of factors.

In mathematics, we often have rules and patterns that converge to make a problem solvable or even impossible to solve. We like using etymology in math, and this is a perfect opportunity. Convergence pairs the prefix *con-*, which means "with" or "together" with the root word *vergere*, which means "to bend, turn, or turn toward." Put them together and you have things that are bending or turning toward each other. This is so lovely in math (and other subjects, of course). Ask, "What step helped your mind bend toward the solution?" or "What parts of the equation are turning towards each other? Which are turning away?"

Let's look at a specific example because we love doing math. Here's our problem: $6 \div 2(1+2) = ?$. We allow students to solve it. What happens? Most students solve it like this: $6 \div 2(1+2) = 6 \div 2(3) = 6 \div 6 = 1$. Except, that's not right. Because of the Order of Operations, we actually have to do the division before we combine that 2 with the contents of the parentheses. Yes, we do the parentheses first, but then we jump back into the PEDMAS order. So, it should be solved: $6 \div 2(1+2) = 6 \div 2^*(1+2) = 6 \div 2^*3 = 3^*3 = 9$. We ask students, "How did our thinking diverge from the Order of Operations? How can we make sure we converge with the Order of Operations? How can we bend our mind towards it?"

It would be impossible to teach social studies well without talking about how people (and ideas) have come together throughout history. The Renaissance was a unique Convergence of people. The American Revolution could not have happened without the coming together of many voices along with factors of time and space. Was the distance between the US and England a required element of this Convergence? The Industrial Revolution was a convergence of ideas and people. Certain circumstances needed to happen at the same time to spark this era. Which factors were essential? Which were optional?

A novel is a convergence of plot, setting, characters, theme, language, and so on. In *The Giving Tree,* how does Shel Silverstein bring each of these together?

How Do I Introduce It to Students?

With Convergence, we want students to understand that the interplay of multiple factors leads to a different result than looking at each individual factor (or Contribution) on its own.

You could introduce this idea with any type of team, whether a basketball team or a team of superheroes or a group of characters in a novel. Each member of the team has their own

Contribution. They *could* play one-on-one or fight the villain on their own. When they come together, however, a team becomes more than the sum of their parts. They can work together, combine their abilities, and do things no one member could have done on their own.

At the same time, there may be new problems that arise when a team Converges. Personality issues, egos, and difficulties in coordinating all arise when a people work together. You could prove the statement, "A convergence of perspectives leads to new solutions and problems" using teams that students come up with. In this way, students can compare how each member of a team of their choosing contributes a unique strength but also adds a complication or weakness.

A Class Is A Convergence

Ian taught at a school that welcomed many new students at each grade level every year. Convergence was a perfect tool for talking about how our class was a result of all these unique perspectives coming together into one place at a certain time.

We'd note what schools each of us started at originally, whose class each of us came from last year, and perhaps even where we had been born. In this way, we bring in elements of Origin and Contribution. But we don't just make a list of who our teachers were last year, we'd discuss the effects of this convergence. Some of us had Mrs. X and some Miss Y. What happens when those pasts come together? Did we learn things in different ways? Will we have conflicts to work though?

When introducing Convergence, make sure to set the expectation that it's not just a list of factors, but an analysis of how those factors worked together.

17

ORIGINS

EVERY SUPERHERO HAS AN ORIGIN STORY. Each product we use began in some interesting way. Every world leader had a first step of their path. Beginnings are interesting. Origin focuses students on the beginning of an idea and the impact that beginning had.

Origin: This, Not That

Early in the book we mentioned the saying, "Well begun is half done." The reverse is also true, which makes Origin really interesting. Sometimes things are broken, and we don't understand why until we go to its genesis.

If you focus only on "How did this start?" when using this Content Imperative, you're using Origin in too shallow of a manner. Origin also has to examine how effective that start was, and it looks at what the implications – predicted and unforeseen – are. Often, we have to beware of too many questions starting with

"What?" With Origin, we have to beware of too many questions beginning with "How?" It's far more than "How did this begin?", although that is certainly part of it.

Interestingly, Origin is being demanded in some content areas now. In math, we're seeing students being asked questions like, "What is the best first step in this problem?" That's Origin. It's essentially asking, "What is the Origin of the optimal solution to this problem?"

> This: In what ways did the characters' first interaction lead to conflict later on?
> Not (Only) This: How did the conflict begin?

> This: In what ways did the experiment's first step influence the outcome?
> Not (Only) This: How does the experiment begin?

> This: In what ways did the ending of WWI become the Origin of WWII?
> Not (Only) This: How did WWII begin?

Origin looks at the foundation of an event, idea, or theory, and it also looks at things that derived from that foundation. What is this thing built upon, and how strong is that foundation? Where did the idea/event then move off into other ideas/events?

We use Origin to explore sources and causes, so we'll see it cropping up naturally in language arts as we look at the root of conflict in stories or the backstory of characters. In a standard plot diagram, the backstory can be labeled "Origin." In social studies we'll use it to look at the changing geopolitical landscape, the ways figures in history emerged, how certain customs developed, and the basis for the governmental structures we see. In science, we'll use Origin to examine catalysts and the foundations of different life forms. In math, we'll use it to look at the basis for solving problems certain ways.

Preconceived notions or biases are also Origin. They sometimes even precede the beginning. Use Origin to guide students to analyze what came even before the beginning and how that influenced the genesis of the event.

Origin can be a powerful tool if we let it be, so avoid staying in the shallow waters with this one. Of course, if you are teaching early elementary, the shallow waters may be appropriate and perfect, but even little ones can sometimes stun us with the quality and complexity of their thinking.

What are Some Sample Question Stems?

Note: We've indicated correlated Depth and Complexity elements in parentheses.

Apply

- What Patterns led to the Origin of solar power? (Patterns)
- What ethical problems exist in the beginning of the frog's life cycle? (Ethics)

- Which Patterns are present during the Origin of a storm? (Patterns)

Analyze

- Compare the Origin of an ethical problem of cell phones with the Origin of a problem with automobiles. (Ethics)
- Consider the possibility that this was doomed from the start. (Details)
- Why would someone want to hide the way this began? (Ethics, Multiple Perspectives)
- What sparked the break-off ____ from ____? (Trends)
- Even though ____ was the technical beginning, what events/beliefs influenced that beginning?
- In what ways is the character not really honest with him/herself about his/her Origin story? (Details)
- How is this Origin story similar/different from that in/of ____ in an important way? (Across Disciplines)
- Describe the Origin of Lincoln's perspective toward the abolition of slavery. (Multiple Perspectives)

Evaluate

- Why is ____ the best first step in solving this problem? (Rules)
- In what ways is the foundation that this idea is built upon broken? (Details)

- Why has the Origin of this become problematic? (Change over Time)
- Was that influence positive or negative? (Details, Ethics)
- Evaluate the influence of the characters' preconceptions on their beliefs and assumptions about the other characters. (Trends)

Synthesize

- Who would be most likely to see this cause as positive/negative? (Multiple Perspectives)
- If this idea is based on an idea that is no longer considered valid, does that invalidate this idea as well? (Ethics)
- In what ways would a different beginning have helped/hurt? (Unanswered Questions)
- How would this have changed if it began in this way [insert alternate beginning] instead? (Unanswered Questions)
- How far after the Origin was it still malleable or changeable? What was the point of no return? (Unanswered Questions, Patterns, Trends)

What are Some Sample Activities?

Anything that students create can explore the Origin of the content. For example, a history teacher could have students create a propaganda-style poster advocating a causal factor in the outbreak of WWII. A science teacher could have students use a graphic organize to illustrate the water cycle and identify the catalyst for evaporation.

Etymology is Origin combined with Language of the Discipline, so anytime you're looking at etymology, you'll use Origin. This is a good example of how the Content Imperative allows you to be more precise. It's not just a definition, you're telling the student. It's how the word or phrase began.

Students can work backwards towards an Origin from a result, or they can be asked to take a catalyst and trace it forward. When you have students start with an Origin and move forward, they can do it with content that is known (where they know both the beginning and the end) or content that is still developing. The latter will allow them to predict a possible outcome.

We can also ask students to use Origin to explore the *why* of their own thinking. When they've made a choice, rather than asking, "Why did you do that?" (In our experience, they can rarely articulate that anyway), you can ask, "Can you identify any of the Origins of that action?" You can dive deeper and ask, "What other paths were possible from that Origin?"

Toyota used a technique called "Five Whys." When they ran into a production problem, they'd ask, "Why did this happen?" Then, when given an answer, they'd ask "Why did *that* happen?" After repeating at least five times, only then would they begin to arrive at the *real* Origin of the problem. You can use this idea with any problem in content. Why did the colonies revolt? Taxation without representation? Why did *that* happen? England needed money? Why? Because of a bungled war? Why did that war happen? And so on. The real Origin can actually be quite surprising!

When you combine Origin with Multiple Perspectives, you ask students to look at not only how different people see things differently, but how those differences began. When you combine Origin with Rules, you ask students to look at not only what rules and boundaries exist, but where they began. What made someone think the boundaries were necessary?

How Do I Introduce It to Students?

Origins is fun to introduce to students because there are so many pop culture references that make it easy. Here's one possible method:

Play a snippet of Michael Jackson's "Wanna Be Startin' Somethin'" to let your get students in the mood to be interested. Of course, if everyone starts dancing, you might want to play the whole song! Explain that you're going to be introducing them to the Content Imperative that wants to be startin' somethin'.

Next, share the backstory on how a few states got their names (be sure to include your own state's naming story).

For example, you could share:

- Idaho is an invented name with an unknown meaning. The man who named it said it was from a Shoshone word, but later said he made it up.

- Louisiana was named in honor of Louis XIV of France.
- Nebraska is named from an Oto Indian word that means "flat water."
- Georgia was named in honor of King George II of England.
- Maryland was named in honor of Henrietta Maria, the queen of Charles I of England. Charles I is the king who got his head chopped off. North Carolina and South Carolina are both named in honor of him.
- No one really knows where the name for Oregon came from.
- Vermont is from the French *vert mont,* meaning "green mountain."

Then show pictures of some superheroes and share their backstory. Here are a few:

- The X-Men: The X-Men were mutants who were born with their abilities and people see them as freaks of nature. Even though they're persecuted, they use their powers to protect the innocent. They are called "X-Men" because they were brought together by Charles Xavier.
- Spider Man: Bullied teenager Peter Parker was bitten by a radioactive spider at a science exhibit.
- Batman: Bruce Wayne was walking home from a movie with his parents when they were held up by a criminal. There was a struggle and his parents were killed right in front of him. Bruce decides to wage war against crime, he trains himself to become Batman.

- Iron Man: Tony Stark was injured and taken captive by enemy soldiers while he was overseas demonstrating some of his amazing inventions. While he was being held captive by the enemy, he built a mechanical suit with the help of a scientist named Ho Yinsen. He then uses that suit to escape and then save the world.

- Captain America: Steve Rogers wanted to serve in World War II, but he was too week and sickly. He was instead chosen for a program called "Project Rebirth" and was injected with Super Soldier Serum that perfected his body. But the scientist who invented it was killed, and the serum's formula was lost. Steve then became the only person ever to get it and he turned himself into Captain America.

Explain that this is called an "origin story" and it tells the backstory that reveals the identity and sometimes even the motivations of heroes or villains.

Explain that the Origin Content Imperative asks us to look carefully at the origin story of the content we're exploring. How did it begin? Why is that beginning important?

If you have students who think deeply enough, you can explore the idea that it's incredibly difficult to define a beginning or separate it from the Möbius strip of time. Play "Circle of Life" from Lion King or Semisonic's "Closing Time" to explore the idea that finding the actual beginning of something is almost always very complex. Every new beginning really does come from some other beginning's end.

When you introduce Origin, make sure you share the depth that is in this Content Imperative. As we warned above, don't let students get caught in the "how" trap, thinking it's only ever asking how something started.

18

PARADOX

PARADOX FOCUSES STUDENTS on the contradictory elements of an idea. How (and why) are there two forces pulling in opposite directions? How can two things that seem to contradict each other both be true? When discussing a Paradox, we look for ideas that cannot exist together, dilemmas, and impossibilities. We look at moral complexity in people and characters. We hold multiple, competing ideas in our minds simultaneously. It is delicious irony.

Paradox: This, Not That

Paradox can be tricky to distinguish from Ethics and Multiple Perspectives, so why not just use them and leave Paradox on the table? The reason is that Paradox is one of the best features of Depth and Complexity for your strongest thinkers. It's the thinking person's Content Imperative.

Paradox is a literary element that we teach in language arts. If you think that it's *only* that, then you're taking too narrow of a view. It's not just about literature, and it appears in virtually all content. If you don't believe us, just search for "paradox" on Wikipedia, and you'll come up with a list that bridges virtually all content areas.

Implementing it effectively requires using good questioning, so it's a great way for a teacher to develop his/her own questioning skills. It's also a great tool for guiding research. Its near obsession with ambiguity makes it perfect for students who are too rigid in their thinking. Forcing them to confront paradoxes broadens their minds. Its purpose is to arrest thought and grab attention, so if your students are really comfortable and relaxed while exploring Paradox, you're probably not going deep enough.

To take full advantage of this, make sure you go beyond merely identifying Paradoxes and ask students to consider how the they got that way. What are the converging Rules, Perspectives, and Ethics that lead to an impossible situation? How does one break through a Paradox? Sometimes we allow a Paradox to linger since no one knows what to do with it. Other times, a strong leader might break through it through force of will.

This: Make the argument that the most effective tool used to resolve this Paradox was _____.

Not (Only) This: What was the Paradox so-and-so faced?

This: If you were to do the experiment again, what could you change to make it more likely to get the expected results?

Not (Only) This: What In what ways did the result of your experiment differ from what you expected?

This: What conditions made it possible for this paradox to exist?

Not (Only) This: Is there a paradox?

You can get students to go deeper with Paradox if you give them the paradox and let them argue it out, rather than always asking them to identify the paradox. You do the identifying sometimes and move them up Bloom's a level.

This: Napoleon was responsible for the deaths of many thousands. Yet he spread the ideals of the French Revolution, including equal rights under the law, and ended the Spanish Inquisition. Argue that he was either primarily good or primarily evil.

Not (Only) This: How was Napoleon both bad and good?

We'll be honest: Paradox is optional. It's next level. It's what you use when you've mastered (or are at least familiar with) the other parts of Depth and Complexity. We're absolutely not saying you need to jump on the Paradox bandwagon right away. We're saying that when the time is right, you will love it.

What are Some Sample Question Stems?

Analyze

- What rule can be bent to lead to a solution to this paradox?
- In what ways were they simultaneously ____ and ____?
- In what ways is this simultaneously good/bad, easy/hard, true/false, light/dark, long/short, big/small?
- Who benefits from this paradox and in what way?
- Why did ____ not act in his/her own best interests?

Evaluate

- Create a list of details that show how wind power, solar power, and fossil rules are each a Paradox in some way. Decide which is the most paradoxical.
- Who in the story do you think exhibits the most complex paradoxical character? In what way does the character's complexity create a struggle for him/her? How does he/she resolve that struggle?
- Some have called the Spanish greedy in their exploration. In what ways is this characterization both true and false?
- What were the three most likely reasons you got different results from that which you were expecting? How could you better control for those results next time?

Synthesize

- When faced with this Paradox, what compromises did people have to make to reach a solution? Were these compromises fair?

- At the beginning, it seemed as though ____ were true, yet we found out that ____ was true as well. Why is it unlikely that both of these things could be true?

- How could this lead someone else to a different conclusion?

- How could that contradiction have been resolved in a different/better/fairer way?

What are Some Sample Activities?

Paradox is the Content Imperative we use when we have results that differ from what we expected. For example, a student follows all of the directions in a lab, yet still has a different result than their peers. When you are creating labs, experiments, problems or scenarios for students, consider how you can increase the likelihood of this happening. Can you make small tweaks that will result in different outcomes that your students can then examine? Create the possibility of paradox.

Use Paradox to create interest in a topic. For instance, if you're teaching students about the Order of Operations for the first time, give them all the same problem and let them work it out before they know the Rule of the Order of Operations. You will likely end up with different answers as they solve the problem out of order.

Use this Paradox - that we all solved the same problem yet achieved different results - as a way to persuade them to the necessity of the concept.

As mentioned, you will also see paradox in literature as one of the literary elements we teach students. This is usually very limited in scope, simply asking students to recognize examples of paradox or select it from a list of choices. That's a shame. Even teachers at very early grade levels can use Paradox to take students deeper than that. Use it to create student interest in texts or to set up a core dilemma.

In *The Great Gatsby*, we're hearing the story through the lens of Nick Carraway, yet he is an unreliable narrator. Our view is skewed because of this, so we both trust and distrust him at the same time. You could teach the entire novel using this angle: trust versus mistrust and the inherent paradox in that dynamic. Consider this strong essay prompt: "In what ways is the trust/mistrust the reader has of Nick's narration similar to the relationships among the characters and they way they trust/mistrust each other? In what ways is Nick the narrator a meta-character? In what ways does the dynamic of trust influence the actions of the characters?" If you're familiar with the novel, you're probably thinking about the ways the different characters both trust and mistrust each other, and how in two instances it leads to death.

Paradox is an author's tool to get the reader's attention or to emphasize a specific idea in the text that might otherwise go overlooked. It's a common technique of the Romantic and metaphysical poets, who often used paradox in their poetry when talking about love and death. It adds emphasis, almost like punctuation. You can use that same power in your classroom, no matter the content area (and even if you're not talking about love or death).

This isn't just for high school. Paradox exists in very early texts. In fact, many fairy tales have paradox as a core premise. Goldilocks is a sweet child, yet she breaks into the home of the three bears and, without permission, steals their food and uses their belongings. This is a great example to combine with Ethics. In *The Cat in the Hat*, the mother returns to a home that seems untouched, yet chaos reigned while she was gone. In her mind, her rule was followed, yet in reality it was not. So, here's a paradox: she thinks the evidence shows her rules were followed, yet they were not. Students – yes, even five-year-olds – can question if the end result is what she wanted, is it important that they didn't follow the rules?

We've mentioned some Depth and Complexity elements that combine well with Paradox, and it combines well with another Content Imperative, too. Having students examine the Origin of the Paradox can be a compelling exercise. At what point did the Paradox become inevitable?

Let's look at a social studies example. Consider the rise of the Nazi party. While Germany (and much of the world) had had a complex relationship with its Jewish population until that point,

Hitler's beliefs led to a complete breakdown of social norms, and resulted in the greatest genocide the world has ever known. Seemingly loving and kind people participated in or ignored the inhuman, often deadly, treatment of their neighbors for years. When did this Paradox – people behaving in ways completely contradictory to their self-professed values – become inevitable? Where was the breaking point?

Here's another one. George Washington is called the father of the United States, yet he had no children. How can someone be a father and simultaneously childless?

Even at very early grades, students can understand paradoxes. When working with Kindergarteners we teach about how people live in different types of houses. Inuit people would use snow to insulate their houses. We can ask students how something cold could be used to keep you warm.

You can use paradox as a sponge activity. Display a paradox and let students ponder it. It's one of the most effective brain teasers available and gets kids thinking. Even if what you're about to learn has nothing to do with the paradox you've shared, you've let them fire up those neural pathways and primed their brains for learning.

Constantly examine your content for the possibility of paradox. Is a character both mean and nice? Does an element behave one way under certain conditions and another way under different ones? Is a leader cruel and kind? Does a problem look easy, while actually being deceptively difficult? Are your classroom rules causing more dissent than they're solving?

How Do I Introduce It to Students?

To Ian, Paradox is perhaps the most fun element of the Depth and Complexity framework to introduce because it gives an excuse to explore many of the delightful paradoxes that humans have thought up. Here are a few favorites:

- Time Travel paradoxes – What if you went back in time and accidentally stopped your grandparents from ever meeting? What would happen to you?

- The Ship of Theseus – If a ship goes on a long voyage and repairs itself along the way so that no original plank of wood remains, is it really the same ship once it returns home? What about if a ship is completely rebuilt on shore? Is *that* the same ship? Are these situations different?

- The Liar's Paradox – Simply ask student to ponder the statement, "This sentence is a lie."

A quick search for paradoxes online will turn up dozens of mind-bending situations where any option seems to be impossible.

Once you've introduced this Content Imperative, this "joke" is essential: "What do you call two doctors?" "A pair 'o docs."

For younger students, ask them to consider how one student could have a great day at school while another student had a horrible day. Let them share ideas for things that would make either a good day or a bad day at school and list them using a T-chart labeled "Good Day" and "Bad Day." Once you have a few ideas on each side, point to the "Good Day" side and say, "This student will go home and tell her mom, 'This was a great day!' The other student will go home and tell his dad, 'This was a terrible day!' Who is right?"

Allow students to come to the idea that both students are correct, even though their conclusions were the opposite of each other.

Another idea that works for older students is to display the line from *Fight Club*, "The first rule of fight club is: You do not talk about fight club." Say, "If you say, 'The first rule of fight club is', you are talking about fight club. So, you've broken the rule by stating the rule." This is called a paradox. It's something that seems contradictory, but isn't.

Then, show the opening lines of Dickens' *A Tale of Two Cities*:

> "It was the best of times, it was the worst of times, it was the age of wisdom, it was the age of foolishness, it was the epoch of belief, it was the epoch of incredulity, it was the season of Light, it was the season of Darkness, it was the spring of hope, it was the winter of despair, we had everything before us, we had nothing before us, we were all going direct to Heaven, we were all going direct the other way."

Ask students if it is possible for these contradictory statements to be true. How can something be both best and worst? How can something be both Spring and Winter? Let them struggle with it a little bit, because Paradox is richer with a little struggle.

Next, show them this statement: "Ignore this email." Discuss if it's possible to do that.

Then, show them the line from Hamlet, "I must be cruel to be kind." Discuss when something that seems cruel is actually kind.

For all of the ideas, end with an explanation that all of these things are paradoxes and in class, we will sometimes use the Paradox Content Imperative to explore things that seem contradictory, yet are true, things that seem at odds with each other, yet are aligned, and results we get that are not what we expected.

19

PARALLEL

"WHY IS A RAVEN LIKE A WRITING DESK?" Lewis Carrol asked in *Alice's Adventures In Wonderland*. This delightfully perplexing analogy is exactly the type of thinking we want from students when we ask them to consider Parallels. We want them to look broadly and find similar ideas, people, or events across content areas and grade-levels. Parallels is all about finding unexpected connections.

Parallel: This, Not That

Parallel ideas should be non-trivial. A bicycle's wheel and the other wheel on the bicycle are indeed parallels, but students should work with more interesting ideas than that. We want unexpected similarities.

Ian's favorite example is to ask students to explore how a human body is a Parallel to a volcano. It sounds impossible at first, but as students start looking closer, they find unexpected connections which lead to a deeper understanding of both the human body and volcanoes (veins are like conduits, magma is like blood, skin is like the crust, and so on). This idea of forming surprising analogies can work with just about any content.

Parallel should purposefully move across content areas. It should force students to practice lateral thinking, making unexpected jumps that open up entirely new possibilities to explore.

What are Some Sample Question Stems?

Analyze

- Looking at three famous leaders from different times, what parallel rules do they follow that make them great?
- Which patterns in the life cycles of frogs, butterflies, and humans show a parallel?
- Identify parallel perspectives in the American Revolution and the US Civil War.
- Explain how exponents, multiplication, and addition are parallel operations.

Evaluate

- Make a list of similarities between X and Y. Which are most surprising?

Synthesize

- What is a parallel attitude towards right and wrong that allow these people to be friends despite other differences?

- Find parallels between a type of mountain and an ancient civilization. What details make each pair similar?

- Find a parallel to this topic using something you studied in the past three years. List the similarities and then come up with a one sentence motto that unites the two ideas.

- Create a parallel math expression that leads to the same solution but uses entirely different numbers and operations.

- X and Y have become friends. What are the rules/details/big ideas that they found in common? (X and Y could be "humans and volcanoes" or "addition and subtraction" or "Caesar and Washington")

What are Some Sample Uses?

Parallel is the part of the framework that forces analogy, even where no obvious analogy exists. This kind of forced, sometimes even counterintuitive, analogy is particularly powerful in developing strong thinking. We're all used to the SAT-type analogies that read, "Shoe is to foot as glove is to ___." But consider how much more powerful the thinking is if we said, "Shoe is to book as coat is to ___." You can probably feel your neural pathways firing up as the brain tries to make sense of something seemingly nonsensical.

Making the Familiar Strange

One activity to practice finding parallels is called "synectics," which sets out to make the familiar strange. It forces students to look at something in a different way than they have before. This idea is from an oldie-but-goodie book called *Patterns and Practices in the Learning-focused Classroom.* Here's how it works:

1. Prepare a four-box organizer (see below).

2. Put students into groups of 3.

3. Next, ask for four items in an assigned category (e.g., commonly found household objects, animals, things found in a forest, recreational activities, foods, etc.). Place one item in each of the four boxes (see below).

4. Reveal the sentence "A _____ is like a _____ because..." Allow groups three minutes to brainstorm sentences using each of the four items at least once. Students should try to complete as many sentences as they can in the time allotted.

5. After three minutes, STOP. The final step is for each group to choose the two sentences they like the best to share with the rest of the class.

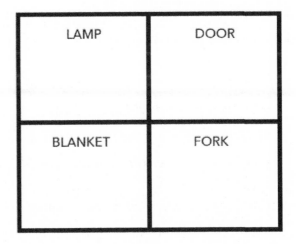

LAMP	DOOR
BLANKET	FORK

The sentence you reveal will be content-connected. So, if you're studying integers, you would write, "An integer is like a ____ because ____." If you're studying landforms, you would write, "A peninsula is like a ____ because____." And so on.

The Jabberwocky Effect:
Language Arts & Social Studies

Lewis Carroll wrote his poem, "Jabberwocky," using made-up words. The reader can still follow the story because the grammar makes sense, even though the lexicon is strange. For example, the first stanza reads:

> *'Twas brillig, and the slithy toves*
> *Did gyre and gimble in the wabe:*
> *All mimsy were the borogoves,*
> *And the mome raths outgrabe.*

It's packed with nonsense words, but plug in the parts of speech, and the English parallels emerge:

'Twas [adjective], and the [adjective] [plural noun]
Did [verb] and [verb] in the [noun]:
All [adjective] were the [plural noun],
And the [adjective] [plural noun] [verb].

If you teach language arts, you could have students create their own versions of Jabberwocky, replacing the parts of speech with substitutes of their choosing. To go further, you could have students add in made-up adverbs, because, for some reason, Carroll didn't do any of those. It's an Unanswered Question!

Social studies teachers could have students write a summary of an historical event using the pattern. For example:

'Twas restless, and the frustrated colonists
Did plan and plot in the towns.
All arrogant were the Kingsmen,
And the shiny guns fired.

This is an example of two different strategies we've discussed. The one we're using here, Parallel, and another we've mentioned elsewhere, constraint. It's powerful because you're forcing broad thought into a narrow structure. It's not just for the humanities, though.

The Jabberwocky Effect: Math

Math teachers can use the Jabberwocky parallel activity, too. We shouldn't be surprised that Carroll, a mathematics professor, would give us a strategy that can be used in math. Consider that in math, we're teaching deep structure. We're not teaching how to solve *this* problem only; we're teaching (hopefully) how to solve *all* of the problems that look like this one. To do that, students must see parallels. They must be able to insert the numbers and operators into unfamiliar structures in order to solve new problems.

Algebra is essentially this same idea. We substitute for x and y. This is the same idea. When you're creating a problem, consider how you can set it up so that students fill in missing parts of an equation. In the same way, language arts students would fill in missing parts of speech. Here's an example:

[even number] + [odd number] = [odd number] – [even number]

Obviously, you could get much more complicated. Let's go a step up:

[integer][exponent][operator][integer]=[integer] x
[integer][exponent]

With word problems, this becomes an even more challenging exercise.

> Your least favorite brother traveled 138 miles to come home for summer vacation, even though you didn't want him to come. He drove for 2 hours and 15 minutes. What is the average speed he was driving? If the speed limit was 55, was he speeding? If so, will you use your amazing math skills to get him in trouble or save the information for leverage later?

Have the students create their own problems, using parallel structure.

> Your [adjective] [relative] traveled [even integer between 108 and 146] miles to come home for [occasion], even though you didn't want him to come. [Pronoun] drove for [number between 1 and 5] hours and [10, 15, or 30] minutes. What is the average speed [pronoun] was driving? If the speed limit was [number], was [pronoun] speeding? If so, will you use your amazing math skills to get [pronoun] in trouble or save the information for leverage later?

The sky's the limit. This is a straightforward way to differentiate for high-ability students. Make sure that you are reinforcing the idea of parallelism – we can substitute numbers and operators while the structure remains the same. Encourage students to look for parallel structures in problems. In what way is *this* problem structured like *that* problem? In what way does *this* set of numbers behave like/unlike *that* set of numbers? In what way does *this* operator function like *that* operator?

Symbol/Picture Analogy

In this activity, we use symbols and pictures to invite students to construct parallels. Here is a list of pictures Lisa uses:

- eagle
- anchor
- light bulb
- ladder
- stoplight
- telephone
- globe
- glasses
- clover
- telescope
- key
- crown
- heart
- suitcase
- bell

- scale
- star
- book

You'd show these images and have students construct parallels. You can do this a couple of ways.

1. Give each student a picture and have them construct the parallel (In what way was solving this problem like a suitcase? In what ways is [our topic] like a key?).
2. Give students a selection of images and have them choose one. Then, they justify their choice: "I choose to say that a pronoun is like a key because it unlocks the connection to the noun." Students can do this activity individually or in groups.

As with the Jabberwocky idea above, be sure to emphasize parallels. How are they similar? If a pattern emerges, bring that element in as well. Parallel works well with Pattern for this reason.

How Do I Introduce It to Students?

A fun introduction are quizzes that ask, "What character from ____ [Star Wars, Harry Potter, etc.] are you?" Take that idea and push it:

- If you were a type of food, what would you be?
- If you were a month of the year, which would you be?
- If you were a movie, what would you be?

Then you could push this idea even further and ask students, "Which character from *Harry Potter* would Han Solo be?" This idea can expand to cross content as well. "Which type of mountain is the best parallel for Ancient Rome?"

So, "Why is a raven like a writing desk?" Lewis Carrol didn't give an answer. But Sam Lloyd offered this parallel: "Poe wrote on both." Ha!

PART IV:

THE REST OF THE STORY

20

Disciplinarianism

THE DEPTH AND COMPLEXITY FRAMEWORK takes the idea of Multiple Perspectives to a new level when we ask students to think like specific experts or (in the language of the framework) disciplinarians. Students learn to approach a topic as if they were in an expert in a specific discipline. They're not just a kid in a math class, but an eight-year old mathematician, using versions of the same tools, language, and questions that an expert would use.

As you teach students to think as disciplinarians, they can approach the same topic from multiple, well-defined perspectives. The American Revolution can be viewed as a geographer, historian, geographer, sociologist, or political scientist would have viewed it. A study of nuclear power could include the viewpoints of a nuclear engineer, an environmentalist, or a local politician.

Defining A Discipline

The Depth and Complexity framework gives us fantastic tools for teaching students to think like experts: the prompts of Depth and Complexity themselves. How would various disciplinarians use the prompts? Whether thinking about a mechanical engineer, a college professor, or a film director, we can teach students:

- the Language they would use
- the Rules they would follow to make their decisions
- the Big Idea they focus on
- the Ethical concerns that experts would worry about
- the Patterns they would rely on

Thinking Like an Economist

Learning to think from a specific expert's perspective means getting to the core of what they study. Often, when you find that core, it becomes obvious that the expert thinks far more broadly than we might at first expect they would.

An economist might use the prompts of depth and complexity like so:

- Big Idea: An economist studies the movement of wealth.
- Ethics: wealth inequality, fraud, poor accounting
- Rules: what is/isn't counted as wealth, laws to follow
- Language: wealth, supply, demand, consumption, production

- Patterns: price increases as demand increases, lower supply can increase demand, too much supply can decrease price

When I asked students to think like economists, I wanted the role to work beyond the most obvious applications. Yes, an economist studies the movement of wealth. Wealth, however, doesn't have to mean money. Any limited resource is wealth. Once my students understood limited resources, we could apply it to content as varied as a novel study and a unit on biomes.

I thought that an interesting question for students to ponder was "What problems is wealth inequality creating" in any given situation. Now, this question is too high-level for many students to start with, so I wrote a series of scaffold questions to guide them to my ultimate goal.

1. What is "wealth" in this situation?
2. Who or what has the most control over wealth?
3. Who or what has little control over wealth?
4. What problems is wealth inequality creating?
5. What may happen if these problems aren't solved?

Consider how this could apply to *The Giving Tree.*

1. Wealth is The Boy's attention.
2. The Boy is in control of his attention.
3. The tree has little control over his attention.
4. The Tree is lonely when The Boy spends his attention on other people or things. She gives him everything in an

attempt to hold his attention, but he is often left alone for long periods of time.

5. In this story, although the ending seems happy since the characters end up together, The Boy still has complete control of his attention. If he decides to up and walk away, The Tree will be left as a mere stump, helpless to regain The Boy's attention.

We could ask the same questions in other situations. In a rainforest, wealth might be sunlight. In *Hatchet*, wealth could be food. In the American colonies, wealth might be control over laws. We could consider how the wealth is spread unevenly and how that creates all sorts of problems.

By carefully defining an economist, we can move students towards a deeper way of thinking within this specific discipline.

Thinking Like Historians

When introducing how historians think, I wanted students to think broadly, going across time and place. Historians see parallels. They know that Hitler's disastrous attack on Russia was remarkably similar to Napoleon's failed invasion. They connect events, people, and ideas in ways that aren't obvious to a novice. This broad thinking might lead them to see that one event may solve a problem but also create new problems. What looks like an ending is also a beginning. Using this thinking, I could break down being a historian using the prompts of Depth and Complexity:

- Big Idea: Historians look at events broadly, noting how they connect across time and place.
- Patterns: Events can solve one problem while creating new problems; endings can also be beginnings; the same kind of events happen throughout history.
- Ethics: An event that appears positive to one group can be a negative for another group.
- Multiple Perspectives: Historians are aware that "winners write history," and we have to look at multiple perspectives in order to fully understand an event.

With that in mind, I had students consider questions such as:

- What factors led to this situation? Which of those factors were most unexpected?
- How well did this event solve a problem? Were there other possible solutions that could have been more positive?
- What unexpected problems did this event lead to? Was the event "worth it" or did it lead to too much future difficulty?
- Is there a similar situation from another time or place? How are the two different?

Note that these questions can apply to history (obviously) but an historian could also read a novel and answer the same questions:

- How well does the fight between Romeo and Tybalt solve a problem? What new problems does it create? Is it similar to any other situations?

- When Meg reunites with her father in *A Wrinkle In Time*, how is this both an ending and a beginning?

Getting Specific

It can help to drill down with your disciplinarians, moving towards either sub-genres of the discipline or specific people who are experts in the field. If I were to break "historian" down, I could look for historians with particular perspectives:

- Howard Zinn, author of *A People's History of the United States*, purposefully surfaces the voices of under-represented people. To think like him, I'd ask students to consider how events in history affected people in poverty, those who couldn't vote, those who couldn't run for office, and so on.

- Mary Beard, a professor who studies Ancient Rome, is careful to note that primary sources are not necessarily reliable and may be infused with the author's bias. To think like her, students should likewise look at a primary source as being potentially unreliable.

The following examples of Philosopher, Engineer, and Author use specifics to generate multiple perspectives within each discipline.

Thinking Like Philosophers

One of Ian's favorite uses of Thinking Like a Disciplinarian is to explore how philosophers think about big problems. We began by defining the perspective of a philosopher generally:

- Big Idea: Ponders the Biggest Ethical Issues of life
- Rules: Not interested in small individual problems, but rather big problems that humans have had for thousands of years.
- Patterns: Notices that many people have the same types of big problems: unhappiness, conflict with others, unsatisfied, even when they get what they want.
- Unanswered question: "*Why* is this a repeating problem?"

I introduced four famous philosophers and defined a Big Idea for each of them. Does this perfectly represent their beliefs? No way. I felt, however, that this struck balance between truth and usability for my class. Feel free to adjust!

- Socrates's Big Idea: Ignorance leads to problems.
- Aristotle's Big Idea: Friendships with selfish purposes create problems.
- Confucius' Big Idea: The young should respect their elders, and elders should be kind to the young.
- Descartes' Big Idea: Begin by doubting all things. Demand proof.

Then, we practiced with simple content. How would each of these philosophers summarize the problems with *The Three Little Pigs*? Kids came up with ideas like:

- Socrates: The pigs are ignorant about their building material, the danger of the wolf, and the need to stay together to survive.
- Aristotle: The pigs don't work together as true friends should.
- Confucius: The mother pig didn't educate her sons well enough.
- Descartes: The pigs were too trusting in their weak materials and in the wolf. If they started with doubt, they would have had more success.

Then, after applying with simple content, we took it to grade-level reading and looked at the conflict in *Hatchet, Where the Red Fern Grows,* and *The Little Prince.*

Thinking Like a Philosopher works naturally in language arts, and it also easily applies to social studies. What would each of these four philosophers think about the problems behind major events from history? How would Socrates see the main problem of World War II compared to Descartes?

Thinking Like Engineers

The 6th grade teachers at Ian's school put on an annual egg-drop competition. While it was always a fun event, it lacked a certain academic rigor that we felt it needed. One year, I applied the Thinking Like a Disciplinarian framework to this science topic and the results were fantastic.

Students formed trios and we defined three disciplinarian-based roles for them to inhabit. I used the elements of Depth and Complexity to define each of these specific engineers. They all had specific Big Ideas, Language of the Discipline, Rules, and Unanswered Questions.

Aerospace Engineers

- Big Idea: Aerospace Engineers are focused on slowing down the structure as it falls to the ground.
- Language: spill hole, line length, chute size
- Rules: A parachute balances material and holes to safely bring an object to the ground.

Structural Engineers

- Big Idea: Structural Engineers are focused on building the outer casing of the egg-drop structure.
- Language: truss, crumple zone, tetrahedron, lattice, geodesic dome
- Rules: The shape of a structure contributes to its strength.

Materials Engineers

- Big Idea: Materials Engineers are focused on using the best materials to fill the structure and cushion the egg.
- Language: compression, loose fill, and inflated packaging.
- Rules: Packing materials balance weight and strength.

When they worked on their egg drop project, each student in the group had specific responsibilities. They knew exactly what to be researching. Their final project was a collaboration of three different types of engineers. And it showed! The change was remarkable when compared to previous years. Every group produced a structure that was high-quality, incorporated parachutes that actually worked, and was filled with interesting materials to cushion the egg. Students could reflect on their peers' creations using high-level language that an engineer would actually use.

By giving students these specific roles, it also allowed us to have "disciplinarian meetings." I could ask all the Aerospace Engineers to join me for a quick lesson or check-in. Or I could have all Materials Engineers find another Materials Engineer from another group and compare notes. In the beginning, since we had three teachers, each teacher took one group of engineers to introduce their specific discipline. Giving students these specific roles opened up many opportunities to increase the thinking (and fun) of this science project.

Thinking Like an Author

"Thinking Like an Author" is just too general to be useful. It lacks direction. Yet when we get highly specific and focus on specific authors, it takes this discipline to a whole new level. When we define a specific author's style, students can practice writing in that style, using long sentences like Charles Dickens, short sentences like Ernest Hemingway, or a bouncy rhythm like Dr. Seuss.

Thinking Like an Author: Older Students

- Ernest Hemingway's Patterns: short sentences, direct, no fluff, more like a journalist
- Zora Neale Hurston's Patterns: colloquial Southern dialect, reads like a folktale, one character (usually the narrator) is lyrical, one character is down-to-earth
- Gabriel Garcia Marquez's Patterns: magical realism (magical elements in a realistic setting), few adjectives or adverbs
- Charles Dickens' Patterns: long sentences, cliffhangers, incredible circumstances

Think Like an Author Tasks

Rewrite these Zora Neale Hurston lines as if you were Charles Dickens:

- Janie saw her life like a great tree in leaf with the things suffered, things enjoyed, things done and undone. Dawn and doom was in the branches.
  "Ah know exactly what I got to tell yuh, but it's hard to know where to start at." (*Their Eyes Were Watching God*)
- Imagine that you are Gabriel Garcia Marquez. Add an element of magical realism to *The Great Gatsby* or *A Tale of Two Cities.*

- Take this Dickens' line and make it over as a Hemingway line:

  "It is a far, far better thing that I do, than I have ever done; it is a far, far better rest that I go to than I have ever known." (*A Tale of Two Cities*)

- Revise a paragraph from *A Thousand Years of Solitude* in the Southern colloquial dialogue of Hurston.

Thinking Like an Author: Younger Students

For younger students, we could define the style of specific authors they are familiar with.

- Dr. Seuss's Patterns: rhyming, predictable rhythm, nonsense words, repeated words or phrases
- Margaret Wise Brown's Patterns: repeated sounds, repeated elements, simple plots

Think Like an Author Tasks

Take a Seuss text like *One Fish, Two Fish, Red Fish, Blue Fish* and replace "fish" with a different noun. Now, leave the "fish" and see if you can replace the adjectives. (e.g., three fish, four fish, roof fish, door fish).

Compare the "if, then" in Runaway Bunny to the "if, then" in *If You Give a Mouse a Cookie*. Advanced students can be invited to rewrite *If You Give a Mouse a Cookie* to read more like *Runaway Bunny*, changing the third person to first person (If you give me a cookie, said the mouse, I'll want a glass of milk...")

Don't be afraid to combine "simple" authors with more advanced content. Ian used a study of Dr. Seuss' style to explain Shakespeare's style, since both authors make extensive use of stressed and unstressed syllables. Students loved unlocking *what exactly* makes Dr. Seuss so Seuss-y and it helped them to more quickly understand iambic pentameter.

Thinking Like a Mathematician

When we ask students to think as mathematicians would, we have to confront the paradox that what students do in math class is rarely like the work that a true mathematician does. A professional mathematician doesn't work through practice problems all day. They don't practice the *known*. They seek to answer unsolved problems.

A big idea might be: Mathematicians apply proven and unproven theories to try to uncover patterns and resolve practical and theoretical questions.

Questions:

- At what point did you first noticed the pattern emerging?
- Which patterns in this problem have you seen in other problems?
- Do you have a name for this pattern yet? Do you need to create a name?
- Why would a mathematician think this were worth solving?
- What shape do you think is a mathematician's favorite?

- How can I communicate this to someone who is not a mathematician?

- Who would solve this type of problem most quickly, a mathematician or a strong reader?

- Is this problem more reader-y or more science-y or more math-y?

- Can you rewrite this word problem to sound like a mathematician wrote it?

- Which is the word a mathematician would be least likely to use to describe this type of problem? Hard or easy? Simple or complicated? Important or unimportant?

- Which theory would a mathematician be most likely to try first when solving this problem?

When we ask students to think like mathematicians, we have to challenge ourselves to give them the kinds of interesting problems that a mathematician would truly face. Ian has collected a set of "Mathematical Curiosities" at Byrdseed.com that are the perfect introduction to the kind of problems that real mathematicians tackle.

Thinking Like a Biologist

The Big Idea of biology is: How do living things interact with each other and their environment?

Questions:

- What does this living thing do that benefits itself but has a negative effect on other creatures or the environment?
- What other living things does this plant or animal converge with? What are the positive effects? What are the negative effects?
- How does a convergence keep this ecosystem in balance? Which one living thing would lead to the biggest change if we removed it?
- How is this convergence different from what each living thing could have done individually? (The whole is different from the sum of its parts.)
- What much smaller or much larger living thing impacts this plant or animal unintentionally?
- What happens if a new creature is introduced or an existing creature is removed?

Thinking Like Geographers

The Big Idea of geographers is that they study the earth's impact on humans and humans' impact on the earth.

Questions:

- What migratory patterns would a geographer notice here? (Patterns)
- Compare the way that a physical geographer would look at the Bantu migration compared to a human geographer?

Whose viewpoint is most important in this instance? (Multiple Perspectives)

- What would a geographer think is the most important implication of the depletion of this natural resource to the biome? (Unanswered Questions)

- Where are three places humans live that geographers would warn them is a bad idea? (Details)

- Which research technique would a geographer use that would most likely result in the needed information, an interview or a review of data? (Unanswered Questions)

- Why would a historian be helpful to a geographer in answering this question? (Across Disciplines)

- Which of the following is having the most impact in this case, economic, social, or political factors? (Trends)

- What laws have been enacted to alleviate human's impact on the environment? What are some of the unintended consequences of those laws? (Rules & Ethics)

- How would a geographer recognize in what ways this biome changed over time? (Change over Time)

Thinking Like Editors

When we ask students to just "edit their writing," it lacks specificity and purpose. Students don't really know what to do. When we frame editing as a discipline, it forces us to think through what we really mean. When we were editing this book, we had to make a checklist of the things we were looking for – we couldn't just say, "Oh, go edit that whole thing." It had to be broken down. We can present the purpose as a Big Idea: "Why edit?" By asking highly specific questions, it helps students to edit more confidently.

The Big Idea of an editor is that an editor improves writing by making it clearer.

Questions:

- Which error is causing the most confusion for the reader?
- Which errors are not important?
- What is the most important line in the essay/story?
- Which paragraph could most benefit from revision?
- What needs to be taken out?

This is another example of a discipline that can be broken down into more specific, sub-disciplines. One year, I created several specific editing jobs for a short story assignment:

- Character Analyst: improves the details of your character.
- Setting Specialist: improves description of your setting.
- Language Lifter: raises simple words to new levels.
- Grammar Maniac: improves simple grammar.

Students had their story edited four times by four different people who were focused on four different problems. Not only that, but I created four specific tasks for each of the jobs to follow. This specificity dramatically improved the editing process and, because they actually knew what to do, my students actually enjoyed editing.

Character Analyst

Seeks to make a character's personality clear through thoughts, actions, and dialog.

- Define the character's specific traits. What are they like?
- Improve dialog to show the character's specific traits.
- Add or improve thoughts that show the character's specific traits.
- Improve actions to show the character's specific traits.

Setting Specialist

Adds interesting words or figurative language that contribute to:

- the setting's visual appearance.
- how the setting sounds.
- how the setting feels.
- how the setting smells.

Language Lifter

Replaces plain or overused words with interesting synonyms.

- Replace plain nouns with interesting and specific synonyms.
- Replace plain verbs with more descriptive verbs.
- Make verbs more interesting by adding adverbs.
- Replace plain adjectives with more specific synonyms.

Grammar Maniac

Pays attention to the correctness of the writing.

- Change simple sentences into complex or compound sentences.
- Adjust extra-long sentences and paragraphs.
- Fix homophone errors.
- Fix run-ons or sentence fragments.

There's So Much You Can Do

We've barely scratched the surface of what you can do with Think Like a Disciplinarian. Our main recommendations are:

- Get specific with your disciplines. Go beyond something as general as "Think Like a Scientist" and define particular types of scientists.
- Use actual people. Rather than "Think Like an Author," we found great success in thinking like Dickens, Seuss, or Hurston.
- Develop specific questions for students to use. Simply saying, "go think like a biologist," is unlikely to change the thinking in your classroom. Give kids scaffolded questions that will take them to a higher level of thinking.
- Go broad. Have students think from different perspective about the *same topic*, including perspectives that aren't obviously related to the topic (How would an economist see a geometry problem in a unique way?).

21

UNIVERSAL THEMES

EVERYONE WANTS TO CONNECT content across subject areas. We all know that teaching isolated facts does not reflect authentic learning. Yes, we have Across Disciplines for individual lessons or units, but how do we create an overarching idea that unifies our content over an entire semester or year? Few of us have a tool to make this happen.

This is why Universal Themes are a key - but tragically underused - part of the Depth and Complexity framework. These powerful, one-word ideas are highly abstract and are designed to connect content across disciplines and grade-levels.

Much of the Depth and Complexity Framework is about helping students to think abstractly. When they find Rules over and over, your class will see that Rules exist in all topics, just in different forms. When students use Details to form a Big Idea, we are moving them towards abstraction. Patterns are also an abstraction formed from Details (but perhaps not as abstract as Big Idea).

Universal Themes take this idea of abstraction even further with one-word concepts that apply to any content area. Common examples of Universal Themes are: power, change, systems, structure, and conflict.

They're each a single word. They're about as abstract as you can get. They each apply to any content you're teaching. And yet they're still simple enough for very young students to wrap their minds around.

Why Abstraction Is Important

Much of students' work at school is on the specific end of the abstract/concrete spectrum. Definitions, dates, formulae, and procedures are all specific to one context. Without a larger idea to hang onto, students forget or mix up these disconnected facts.

We learn better when we can fit the concrete and the abstract together. In literature, we connect books by their themes, genres, or time-periods. In history, we group events and people together into eras or movements. In science we group similar ideas into larger concepts, from types of mountains, to clouds, to elements on the periodic table. In music, we group individual notes into chords, scales, and keys.

Jerome Bruner (Ian's edu-crush) wrote that connecting facts to abstract ideas prepares students for connections in future lessons. Any single, isolated fact's usefulness is relatively limited.

When we attach those facts to larger concepts, however, it paves the way for learning still to come. Bruner called this "Future Applicability."

Ian's sixth grade students came in already using phrases like "I see an ethical problem" and "This is an example of a system" because their previous teachers had paved the way for future learning by using the Depth and Complexity framework. By teaching with larger, more abstract ideas, we give students a context that makes future learning easier.

Abstraction enables connections. If you've ever heard a student say, "Oh this reminds me of..." and then makes some totally unexpected relationship, they're making an abstraction that connects two (seemingly) isolated facts.

This is a powerful mode of thinking that must be practiced. We must build in regular opportunities for students to think at various levels of abstraction.

This is why Universal Themes are so powerful. Universal Themes are *so* abstract that they can frame *any* topic you teach (seriously). In fact, a Universal Theme is only "universal" if it's, well, *universal!* It must apply to any topic.

Universal Themes: This, Not That

Folks get the scope wrong. They call an idea like "Hero's Journey" their Universal Theme. "Hero's Journey" is indeed a theme, but only in literature. It is definitely not a *Universal* Theme since it doesn't apply to any topic in any grade. Sure, you can make *some* connections, but "Hero's Journey" is a theme that works primarily in one subject. That doesn't mean it's bad. It is indeed abstract, but just not abstract enough to be "universal."

In the same vein, teachers decorate their board to look like a forest, read a book about forests, and teach a lesson about forests and then call that a theme. "Forests" is not even close to a Universal Theme.

For folks who actually are using a true Universal Theme, it's a common mistake to try using multiple Universal Themes at once. Because the purpose of a Universal Theme is to connect as much content as possible, you should use only one theme for the whole year.

The final mistake, and one that I made, is to forget about the theme throughout the year. In order for the Universal Theme to serve its purpose, it must be a constant. It's better to have a once-a-week, ten minute check-in with the theme than to forget about it for two months and then jam it in everywhere and then forget about it again.

Pick Your Theme

Some teachers just pick one theme and use it year after year. Others switch it up from one year to the next. At Ian's school, we were assigned our Universal Theme. Each grade rotated through the themes in such a way that students would never repeat one, even if they were at our school for six years.

The Themes

There are various versions of the list of Universal Themes floating around out there. Some have as many as ten possible themes. We're going to focus on these options: power, systems, change, conflict, order, and force.

Power

When we ask students to think about Power, their natural inclination is to focus on physical strength or a super-power. Throughout the year, you will help them to expand their understanding of power.

When using this theme, it's common to use the phrase "Power can take many forms" and highlight that power can be indirect, invisible, and subtle as well as giant and explosive. Power might take the form of electricity, heat, money, a loud voice, or a kind smile.

The generalization "Power can influence" gets students thinking about how what appears to be all-powerful might be controlled by something that seems less significant. Which has more power, a crane operator or the actual crane?

I personally loved the generalization, "Power can be seen or unseen" because it emphasizes the more subtle forms of power. Here in the classroom, what power is seen and what is unseen?

Example prompts related to power:

- Who has the most power, a lobbyist, a politician, or a voter?

- Is a virus more powerful than a gorilla?
- Which mathematical operation is most powerful?
- Which has more power: nouns or verbs?

Systems

When you use Systems as your Universal Theme, students will be thinking about interlocking parts and how one idea interacts with other ideas in predictable ways. They might start with clearly physical systems, like a watch or an engine, in which we can see the parts connecting and working together. You'll want to move them towards thinking about systems in which the interlocking parts do not connect together in such an obvious manner. The human body is a system, a school is a system, and a sentence is a system.

A common generalization to start with is simply "Systems contain parts." For a watch, those parts are obviously the gears. A human body's parts include bones, muscles, and organs. A school's parts might be classrooms, teachers, and students. A sentence is a system made up of words and punctuation.

I love the generalization "A system can contain other systems" because it moves kids up and down a spectrum of systems. School, for example, is a system of classrooms, but each classroom is also a system. Then we could get larger. A school is, itself, a sub-system within a school district, which is also a system within a larger government system and so on. Likewise, the human body contains other systems and sub-systems. A sentence contains clauses and forms paragraphs and other larger systems.

The simple generalization "Systems interact" moves students towards thinking more broadly. A school interacts with a city's other systems, such as the electrical grid, sanitation, and transportation. A school may occasionally interact with the police or the fire department.

Systems can include:

- Mechanical systems: watches, engines, trains
- Electronic systems: circuit boards, tubes, wiring
- Systems of humans: teams, families, political parties
- Systems within humans: cardiovascular, digestive, respiratory
- Natural systems: weather, oceans, ecosystems,
- Mathematical systems: an equation, a graph, a geometric figure
- Intellectual property: the Star Wars universe, the Marvel Cinematic Universe, the Harry Potter universe

Change

When you focus on the Universal Theme of "Change," students learn to see that any topic is in a state of flux. You might start by bringing in pictures of yourself when you were younger. Kids will want to talk about the obvious physical changes, but you might emphasize how you have changed emotionally or how you've changed beliefs and interests. I'd emphasize how I'm still changing even though my body won't grow any taller.

The generalization "Change leads to more change" is one of my favorites. As I grow and learn new things, those changes naturally cause more changes. When the weather goes from cool to warm, it's not just the temperature that changes. Plants, animals, and even buildings react. And *those* changes lead to still more changes.

Applied to math, students might note that if they change a vertex of a shape, it also changes the length of two sides. If they change one piece of an equation, they must also make an equal change to the opposite side. When they change the quotient of a division problem, it changes the solution. I recently read about the Greek's belief that *one was not a number!* Here is a core mathematical belief that has changed over time.

The prompt Change over Time is for more specific questions. The Universal Theme is an overarching idea that we use to anchor everything we're studying. No matter what, we're looking at change.

Conflict

When conflict is your Universal Theme, students will picture two people having an argument. We want to expand their thinking towards the more general idea of two forces pushing against each other. In fact, the generalization "Conflict comes from opposite forces" will be helpful in focusing students on this way of thinking.

Those two forces could be internal, like when Mr. Byrd's immediate desire to eat an entire pizza goes against his larger desire to be healthy. Perhaps I hear a new idea that conflicts with my worldview. These are two forces pushing against each other. Conflict can be seen in nature, as the force of a wave crashes against the force of a rock. We can see forces in history going up against each other in the form of different groups of people. When we approach a math problem, our desire to be done quickly smashes against the complexity of the problem.

Conflict between people doesn't have to be a screaming argument or even tinged with negative feelings. People can strive for two different ideas and remain friendly and positive (as your two authors have done numerous times while working on this project!). The generalization "Conflict can lead to growth" highlights this unexpected side of conflict. When we struggle, we improve. When a country goes through a difficult period, something new comes out. When a butterfly emerges from a cocoon, that conflict has led to growth.

Order

When your Universal Theme is Order, students will explore the balance between predictable patterns and the inevitable disruption of those patterns. Examples of Order will probably start with explicit laws and rules, but you'll want to move students towards thinking of types of Order that emerges without being purposefully designed.

A useful generalization for this purpose is "Order can be natural or constructed." Humans can certainly create order, but the equilibrium of predators and prey is an example of order that arises without an explicit rule. This order just... happens. The balance of planets, satellites, asteroids, and the sun is an example of order that the solar system itself has found.

Interestingly, much Order is temporary. Eventually, the balance of predators and prey will be tipped in some way. The gravitational pull of the sun will overcome the momentum of the planets' orbits. Humans' rules become outdated and people protest or revolt. Order leads to disorder.

In some classrooms, this theme is actually called Order and Chaos. A favorite generalization of mine is "Order leads to chaos and chaos leads to order." I guarantee you students will be able to cite examples of their own home when too much order has led to disorder and vice versa.

If a species develops a new defense, it may disrupt the existing order. When a planet gets away from its orbit, the solar system will lose its equilibrium. However, this inevitable disorder will eventually lead to a new balance. Likewise, humanity reaches decades of order only to be disrupted by revolutions or new inventions. Then, it may take decades to settle into a new order.

This movement from order to chaos back to order and so on can be captured in the generalization "Order has repeating patterns." Our school day is ordered along a set of repeating patterns, but human history is also a larger example of repeating patterns, and perhaps a study of plate tectonics is an even larger example of the same idea. Ian's friend, Araceli, used the Will Durand quote, "A civilization begins with order, grows with liberty and dies with chaos" as an example of repeating order in social studies that specifically includes devolving into chaos.

Math itself is a study of finding Order from chaos. If you'd like to introduce the idea of order using math, Pascal's Triangle would be an intriguing place to begin. How many examples of Order are present? What are the repeating patterns that appear? As you browse Pascal's Triangle, do you have moments of chaos, where you lose the patterns?

How Do I Introduce It to Students?

On the first day of school, Ian introduced his Universal Theme by having students brainstorm as many examples of that theme as they could. We'll use "power" as the sample theme here, but this framework would work with any of the Universal Themes. This whole model is based on Hilda Taba's idea of Concept Formation, by the way.

I'd ask, "What are some examples of power? You can think of things from home, school, from movies, books, games, whatever you'd like. Power exists *everywhere!*" I'd write (or type) these down as fast as kids could come up with them.

Our goal was to get 50 specific examples of power. Yes, this meant we'd sit through moments of awkward silence (tell kids this is ok up front), but someone would always break through with a new direction that would get us five or ten more ideas. The longer you go and the more awkward silences you wait through, the greater variety of examples you'll gather.

This is a blast. You get to learn lots about your students, they get to see that you're open to off-the-wall thinking, and you get to set the precedent that you're patient and not the type of teacher who says, "We don't have time." We *always* have time to think.

When we'd brainstorm examples of Power, kids always started with bland ideas like "electricity" and "wind." After twenty-minutes, however, we'd have examples like "Jackie Chan's feet" or "my mom's face when I am too loud." Yes! Now we're talking.

Then, once you have enough examples, it's time for phase two. Students will form categories from their specific examples. I don't begin with that instruction, however. Instead, I say "What are two examples here that you think are related? Let's make a pair." When you get a response, mark these with a shape or color (or a colored shape!). Something to categorize the pair, but without an explicit label yet (we want to keep thinking flexible and an official label will shut down that flexibility). I'd ask for a second pair of examples that go together. Perhaps a third. Then I'd ask students to add a third example to one of the existing pairs. We'd start to make little groups.

For example, students might make the following pairs: wheels and feet, lightning and earthquakes, and money and politicians. Then they might add "trains" to the "wheels and feet" group.

As soon as they understand what we're doing, I'd put everyone into small groups or three or so and give them this instruction: "Now put *all* of our examples of power into three to five categories. You can use the ideas we started with or you can begin with a blank slate." I'd ask them to avoid making an 'other' group, since I felt it was a cop-out. In the end, they'd create a one- or two-word label for each of their groups.

Perhaps the "wheels, feet, and trains" group grows to become "Transportation."

While they make their groups, I'd walk the room, clarifying directions and observing, but never ever indicating whether I think their idea is "good" or not. I don't want to influence their thinking (this is very annoying to some students who want to be told they're "doing it right").

Eventually, everyone has formed three to five categories of examples and given each category a label. Even though everyone starts with the same examples, we always a get a huge variety of category labels. It's so fun to see how each group thinks differently about which items are related. As we wrap up this phase, I'd have students share their categories. I'd explicitly point out that these categories are more specific than the Universal Theme of "power," but less specific than the examples we brainstormed. They're a middle level. We want students to be comfortable moving between various levels of abstraction.

The final stage of a Concept Formation lesson is to ask students to generate a statement about the Universal Theme that incorporates the category names. This step really gets brains sweating. Sometimes students create a list ("Power can come from our bodies, our minds, or our feelings.") which is fine, but I'd also push those students to see if they can reform their idea into a statement (for example, "The power of our bodies is controlled by our mind and feelings."). This doesn't always work, but it's worth the extra effort.

We'd whip around the room and share these statements about power. I'd type them all out and post them in the classroom, give each student a copy, and make sure that these statements become part of our class vocabulary. I'm going to reference these ideas as much as possible when I teach throughout the year ("Hey, this is an example of our statement that our mind and feelings have power over our bodies!").

Generalizations

These statements about the Universal Theme are called "Generalizations" in the Depth and Complexity framework. They're sentence-sized and, while abstract, are not as abstract as the theme itself. "Power" can apply to anything, but "Power can be used or abused" may not always work in every situation – and that's fine.

In this opening task, students have actually created their own Generalizations. There's also a set of pre-made Generalizations for each of the Universal Themes. For Power, you'll find ideas like:

- Power can be seen or unseen.

- Power can be given, earned, or taken away.
- Power can be used or abused.

Each year, my students would get a sheet that included both the pre-made Generalizations and the ones they created. I'd post that sheet on the walls as well. I tried to create an expectation that we'd be using these ideas constantly.

Other Intro Ideas

If you wandered the halls of Ian's school, you'd see evidence of Universal Theme introductions in every classroom, from first through sixth grade. Some teachers go visual. They ask students to bring in pictures of the theme. Just like my brainstorming, the idea is to get a wide variety of examples of Power or Structures or Systems. Then, after sharing their pictures, the class cuts them out and pastes them together to form a giant word "Systems" built out of systems that the teacher would hang prominently on a wall.

Other teachers went kinesthetic: they passed out a bunch of "junk" (paper cups, napkins, straws, paper towel rolls, and so on) and gave groups limited time (say fifteen minutes) to "build the theme." Kids had to quickly decide how best to show "Change" using their meager supplies. Naturally, everyone would go around and explain why their pile of junk represents "Change."

Other classes had students build PowerPoint presentations with examples of the theme or students could introduce how the theme is present in their lives.

However you choose to introduce your Universal Theme, these first couple of days are all about helping students not just understand the meaning of the theme, but to see that it is present in every topic. It's vital to start well with the Universal Theme, but it's equally important to keep it fresh. Use your Universal Theme regularly or the class will forget about it.

Applying the Theme Year-Round

Look for Examples

The simplest way to keep the Universal Theme in students' mind is just to ask them to constantly look for examples of the theme. After reading a chapter of *Hatchet*, we'd jot down the examples of power we saw: the porcupine, the fire, Brian's courage, the weather, and so on.

This is a fine starting place, but note that it relies only on the bottom of Bloom's taxonomy. We're just asking for students to list examples. Try to move the thinking skill up as students gain familiarity with the Universal Theme.

Comparing and Evaluating

They might have to explain which story demonstrates Power in the most unexpected way: *Hatchet* or *The True Confessions of Charlotte Doyle.* Which was more Powerful, Ancient Rome or Ancient Greece (or Athens vs Sparta)? Which part of the electromagnetic spectrum is most Powerful?

We could also use Systems in the same way. Which protagonist set up the best System to lead to success? Which civilization had the best Systems?

These questions get students analyzing and evaluating. Another way to ensure that you're moving away from only listing examples is to bring in those Generalizations.

Prove or Disprove A Generalization

Choose a Generalization about your Theme and ask students to prove it or disprove it using evidence from a lesson or unit.

When Power was my theme, I'd often ask students to prove or disprove the generalization "Power can be seen or unseen" in topics ranging from ancient civilizations and literature to earth science and math. We'd make two columns: evidence for and evidence against. They'd fill those columns with Details from our lessons. Then they'd decide if the Generalization really applied or not.

If you're using Change, you might finish a unit on the Age of Exploration, then ask students to show whether "Change can lead to more change" is true or false in this context. Such a task is a perfect way to differentiate. While some of your students work with an on-level task, others can prove (or disprove) a Generalization.

You should take this idea across content often. Perhaps at the end of each month, ask students to prove that "Systems contain other systems" using evidence from their recent math, language arts, science, and social studies lessons. My students liked having a "my life" category as well to bring in ideas from outside school.

How It Benefits Teachers

One year, Lisa was teaching *Romeo and Juliet*. Again. As she opened her mouth to begin her spiel for the third time that day, instead of her engaging, carefully designed activity to lure kids into loving the play, what came out was not what she'd planned. "This is an overrated play about a couple of teenagers," she said. "They hook up at a party and it causes all kinds of problems. At the end, it becomes obvious that neither of them paid attention in biology, because they can't tell who's alive and who's dead, and they both end up dead. The end."

It was not a pedagogical highlight in her career. The truth was, she was sick of teaching the same play over and over and over again. Had she chosen a Universal Theme for the year like Ian had, she could have looked at the play through one lens one year and a different lens the next. This would have prevented burn out, or at least minimized it. Imagine looking at the play through the lens of systems one year and then power the next. She wants to teach it again just thinking about it. Don't be like Lisa. Be like Ian.

Teaching with Universal Themes

You can also bring Universal Themes and Generalizations directly into your teaching. It can look as simple as this: teach your lesson as normal, but take one minute in the beginning to introduce a Generalization of your choosing and end by bringing the generalization back to students' minds.

For example, I'd open a lesson about animals' life cycles by saying, "As we learn about life-cycles today, I want you all to look for examples of how 'Change can lead to more change.'" Then I'd teach the lesson. In the end, I'd ask students, "Did anyone see any examples in this lesson of how 'Change can lead to more change'?" This takes very little time but gives students the opportunity to practice making larger connections.

Naturally, you can integrate the generalization and theme more tightly into your lesson-planning if you'd like. I found that this focused my teaching in a way I really enjoyed. I used the phrase "Power can be seen or unseen" in all of my Earth Science lessons. As I taught, I built the lessons around this statement. It worked beautifully. My rather disjointed science content of earthquakes, weather, heat transfer, the electromagnetic spectrum, and food webs all had a common connection. I even assessed my students using this generalization. They'd write an essay after each unit proving or disproving that "Power can be seen or unseen." My students enjoyed the structure these statements gave our content.

When we empower students to move up and down the spectrum of abstraction, we increase their depth of learning, encourage unexpected connections, and prepare the way for future learning.

22

THE FRAMEWORK IN THE EARLY ELEMENTARY CLASSROOM

WHENEVER WE'RE FACILITATING a training on Depth and Complexity, one of the common questions we're asked is "How does this work with Kindergarteners?" The idea behind this question is often that Depth and Complexity seems too complicated, too sophisticated for our itty-bitties. Nothing could be further from the truth. Depth and Complexity works equally well with very young students, and in this chapter, we'll explore that a little bit more deeply.

Throughout the book, we've shared examples and strategies any teacher could use, yet the frequency of the question of how to use it with younger students makes us think that a chapter devoted just to those early grades may be useful to some of you.

Start Small

Look, you don't need to use all eleven elements, all five Content Imperatives, pick a Universal Theme and consider fifteen different ways your students can be Disciplinarians. Just pick two or three elements and start there. How do you choose? Make a list of the most common things you teach. Probably language arts and math. What's math? Patterns and Rules. What's language arts in early grades? Patterns and Rules. Ta-da! You've got your first two elements. Start with those. Use them long enough for the students to become both familiar and comfortable with them before you even consider adding more.

There is no law that says you ever need to use all eleven elements. If you only use four or five the whole year, that's fine. No pressure. There's no right answer for which ones you should use, so be discriminating about what works best for you. The next year, you may add a little more and a little more and a little more. There's no rush.

Go Slowly, One Element at a Time

When you're ready to add new elements, go slowly. Introduce a new element and wait awhile – maybe even weeks! – before adding in another. It's not a race. You know those (annoying) recipes that make you cream the butter and sugar and then add the eggs one at a time? Yeah, do that. Go slowly. Mix in a new element thoroughly before moving on to the next one. There is no timeline for when they need to be introduced, and there's no prescribed order, either. Go slowly, pick what works for you, and know that if your students' thinking is improving, you're doing it right.

How do you know what element to add next? Add the element you need.

It sounds like an oversimplification, but it's true. As you are creating a lesson or looking at a lesson provided for you in your curriculum, open your mind to how the students might benefit from the addition of another element to the ones they've learned. You can do this from three perspectives: the content, the standard, or the one you like.

Content

Let's go with the content first. Let's say you're working with a story on mammals. You might like to introduce the Details element so that your students can discuss the Details of what makes an animal a mammal. You'd want the same if you were reading the poem "Mix a Pancake" by Christina Rossetti. If you're reading *Are You My Mother?*, you may wish to introduce Unanswered Questions. In these examples, the content leads you to the element. You fit the elements to the content, not the other way around.

Standard

If you want to approach from the standard, look at the standard you want to teach and consider which element matches it best. If you're looking at a math standard that wants students to be able to say the number names in order and/or understand that the last number name spoken tells the number of objects counted or one that wants students to name shapes, that's Language of the Discipline. In this case, we look at the standard and ask, "What element would help me teach this?" Remember: Depth and Complexity is a tool for you to use, not a weapon wielded against you.

What You Like

Another option is to pick an element you like and introduce it. We love Ethics the most of all, and we'd definitely use this with little ones. They are obsessed with fairness and justice, so it's a great fit. If you're reading *Mr. Popper's Penguins* aloud, you could discuss the fairness of keeping penguins in a house instead of where they usually live. If you're teaching decomposing numbers into pairs, you could talk about what problems we encounter when we try to do that. Frankly, there is nothing we can think of that five- and six-year-olds aren't willing to tell you if they think it's right or wrong, fair or unfair. Pick the element you like the best and go for it. If you like it, chances are your students will pick up on that feeling, and they'll like it, too.

Linger Longer

With our younger ones, we stay with the same element longer. Think about how you'll spend a whole week on something, revisited -am words over and over. The same model works for the framework, too. Let's say you've introduced the Patterns element.

During the course of a week, you could return again and again to this element as you looked at:

- The way we follow words from left to right, top to bottom, and page by page
- How words have spaces between them
- Rhymes
- The patterns of what plants and animals need to survive (NGSS standard K-LS1-1 has the word "patterns" written right into it).
- During morning meetings, discuss weather patterns. Have we had a series of cloudy or sunny days? When do we think the pattern will be broken?
- Composing shapes
- Similarities in shapes. How are squares and rectangles similar? How are they different?

Repetitively using the same element for a longer period of time solidifies understanding of the element. This is deeper than the "go slowly" we mentioned above. It's not just that you add the elements slowly; it's that you come back to them again and again in a concentrated period of time. As long as you are doing this with varied content, it will not feel boring.

Practical Examples

While we hesitate to give too many specifics because we don't want to sound like there is one right way, we know that people want to see specific examples. Please keep in mind that we are not saying that these are the only way, just some samples.

Introducing Books

One task we often ask of students is to make predictions. We do this particularly with showing the cover of a book and asking them what they think the book is about. Don't just ask, "What do you think this book will be about?" Jazz that up a little bit with Depth and Complexity. If you use different elements each time, it keeps the exercise from becoming same-y and repetitive. Here are some examples of what we mean (this will depend upon what elements your students have been exposed to and what fits the specific book):

- What words give us a clue about what this book will be about? (Language of the Discipline)
- What other book does this book make you think about? (Across Disciplines)
- Who do you think is most likely to pick this book up at the library? (Multiple Perspectives)
- Do think this book is going to be more about this or that? (Multiple Perspectives)
- When do you think this book happened? (Details)
- How many characters do you think this book will have? (Details)
- What other color do you think would have looked good on this cover? (Multiple Perspectives)

- Where is the author's name on this book? (Details)

Help Students Look at Content

Imagine that you have just studied houses. I'm choosing this because in my state, both Kinder and first grade look at the idea that people live in houses and communities. With Depth and Complexity, I can make it more likely that students will give quality responses when I try to check for understanding because I can divide responses by element. For example, after we've studied houses, I can ask:

- What are the Rules houses have to follow?
- What are important Details about houses?
- What are some of the words we use to talk about houses? (Language of the Discipline)

Why this is such a useful exercise is that constraint – narrowing down the possible thinking – actually leads to better thinking. Sometimes, a question can be too wide open to lead to great responses. Depth and Complexity can help narrow the thinking in a way that will open it up. It's a paradox. See what we did there?

Help Students Write More Creatively

If you've already read the chapter on Multiple Perspectives, you know that one of our favorite things to do is to have students view something through the "eyes" of an inanimate or non-human object. Have students write from this perspective. How does:

- the blacktop feel at recess?

- a pencil feel when it is writing?

- a pair of shoes feel when they are not the ones chosen to be worn?

- a flower feel when a butterfly lands on it?

- a bear feel when it wakes up from hibernation?

- the world feel to see the bears waking from hibernation?

- the equals sign feel?

- a really big number feel when someone counts to it?

- a circle feel when it becomes a sphere?

- a house feel when it is being built?

Help Students Make Frames

Even young ones can use frames, so be sure to look carefully at Chapter 24. Remember that frames are about the question that accompanies each section, not just putting an icon in the section and calling it good. This is especially important with our younger students. Two things will help them be able to approach frames:

1. Questions that are appropriate for their ability
2. Lines in the sections to write on.

You may even wish to consider putting in lines with dashes at the x-height. We've got one in the digital resources at giftedguild.com/dcextras.

Let's say you're going to have your students create a frame about summer vacation. Choose four elements you know your students are familiar with. For this illustration, we'll use Unanswered Questions, Multiple Perspectives, Language of the

Discipline, and Rules. We'd choose the style of frame like, put the icons we're using in the corner of each section, and then give these questions:

- Unanswered Questions: What do you think will be your favorite thing you'll do this summer?

- Multiple Perspectives: How do you think your backpack feels about summer vacation?

- Language of the Discipline: What are five words you will use during the summer that you don't use as much during school? Which of those words is your favorite?

- Rules: Why do you think parents have different rules in the summer than during school? What are some rules that are different in your home during the summer?

In the center, you can have them draw a picture of something they'll do that summer.

We'll give another example. Math this time. Mostly, this is the same process. Pick a piece of content and a frame style. Choose four elements. Write four questions. Decide what goes in the middle. Let's say we're going to have them do a frame about squares. To illustrate that all of the elements work with little ones, we'll choose different ones from the frame above. This time, we'll use Details, Across Disciplines, Trends, and Ethics. Here are our questions:

- Details: What are three things that are true of squares that are not true of circles?

- Across Disciplines: Who would need a square more, someone who builds houses or someone who builds bridges?
- Trends: If a square is getting bigger, what is happening to the sides? What is happening to the angles?
- Ethics: Is it fair to call a rectangle a messed up square?

If you see a question and think, "Oh, my students couldn't think of anything to say to that," you can do two things. You can try and perhaps be surprised, or you can choose another question. If you're nervous, just ask super simple questions like, "What are you going to do this summer?" (Unanswered Questions) or "What are three things you want to do this summer?" (Details).

We Recommend

If you teach Kinder or first grade, we highly recommend the website notjustchildsplay.blogspot.com. This website is a deep dive into the classroom of Texas Kindergarten teacher Joelle Trayers. She is not only an amazing Kinder GT teacher, but she is an expert at using Depth and Complexity with little ones. The site is chock-full of specifics, including pictures of student work. Because the site does not have categories, the best way we've found to discover the Depth and Complexity activities is to expand her Archives on the right and look at the titles of the articles. You'll see the elements and the word "frames".

We reached out to Joelle to ask her to share a message to other teachers of our younger students, and she wrote:

I am a Kindergarten teacher who is passionate about rigor and incorporating activities daily that will challenge my students. Years ago, I attended a training about Depth and Complexity and was inspired to get back to my classroom and try out these ideas.

My favorite concepts to introduce to my Kindergartners are Ethics and Multiple Perspectives. I do both with literature and in our reading response activities. After studying ethics my students learn how to create an argument for their opinions, rather than just trying to say the answer they think the teacher wants to hear.

Multiple Perspectives helps students develop empathy and the ability to put themselves in another's shoes. It is so easy to use these concepts with the stories and writing activities you are already planning to feature in your lessons.

Whenever I present my ideas the one thing I always emphasize with teachers of little ones is: you will get the best results if you include these activities into your daily curriculum. Teachers have told me they tried an activity and the kids just didn't seem to get it. This is often the first time we are requiring these early childhood students to really think and apply what they are learning in a different way. Don't give up. The more often you incorporate these concepts the more you will see them grow. You will be amazed to see what your students can come up with when you challenge them.

Ready to Get Started?

To get started, we'd suggest looking through the next few weeks of your upcoming lesson plans. Just skim them, looking for any elements that jump out at you. Choose one and re-read the chapter on it, preparing to introduce it to students. Next, look closely at the lesson plan and write questions that use the prompt you chose. That's all. Start simply. No need to make a big production of it. Just start with questions.

When you're ready to go to the next level, consider incorporating an activity, such as using a graphic organizer with an element. You can also add in a new element. Once you have two, you can do Venn diagrams.

One thing you can do is to use the language of the prompt before you actually teach it. For example, if you're talking about the main idea of a story, you can say, "So what do you think this story is all about? What's its big idea?" Just use the name naturally. Then, when you feel the time is right, introduce it more formally by saying, "You know how when we've been talking about stories and I've asked you what the story was about, what it's big idea was? Well, that's a new element we're going to be using called Big Idea."

It's that simple. Just start. It'll be just fine. Your students are capable of pretty incredible thinking, and Depth and Complexity will help them show it off.

23

THE FRAMEWORK AND GRAPHIC ORGANIZERS

WE LIKE GRAPHIC ORGANIZERS in general because research shows they reduce cognitive demands on students. That frees their brain space for deeper thinking. (We've listed some of those studies in the References section of the Appendix, if you'd like to check that out.)

Graphic Organizers: What They Must Do

There are formal, familiar graphic organizers like the Venn diagram and Thinking Maps, but at their simplest form, graphic organizers use lines, circles, and boxes to help students visually organize information. If a graphic organizer is used for a purpose other than helping students organize thinking, then it's not doing its job. Because they help students organize their thinking, we like to consider graphic organizers as a form of scaffolding.

Graphic Organizers: This, Not That

We see graphic organizers used as a substitute for others product students might create, like a worksheet or a simple list. If all the graphic organizer is doing is making information look different, then that's not enough. Graphic organizers should help students demonstrate cause and effect, compare and contrast information, or make unexpected connections. They may also help organize information that repeats or occurs in a linear sequence (Ellis & Howard, 2007). Be intentional about the purpose of the graphic organizer before you start combining it with Depth and Complexity prompts. Graphic organizers are not about looking nice, they're about pushing students' thinking.

> This: Draw three circles and fill them in with the stages of the life cycle of the plant. Consider this pattern. Which part of this pattern is most easily observed by someone driving by a forest? Which part of the pattern is the most impacted by drought?
>
> Not This: Fill in this diagram with the different stages of the life cycle of the plant.

Another mistake teachers make is to stop too soon. The graphic organizer should be a stepping stone to a more robust product, even if that product is a quality Big Idea (you'll see examples below). When a graphic organizer is an end unto itself, we've left the task half-done. The thinking is incomplete. It's a dress rehearsal with no performance.

This: Using the ideas from your completed graphic organizer, write a paragraph justifying your position on the issue of _____. (Multiple Perspectives)

Not This: Complete this graphic organizer.

Just like depth and complexity icons themselves, we believe students should draw their own graphic organizers. Their task becomes less about "fill in the blanks my teacher gave me" and more about their own thinking. They can also adjust their organizer's size more easily.

Venn Diagrams

We use Venns to help students make comparisons and find differences. Add in Depth and Complexity and we can go deeper. Rather than just asking students to compare and contrast Washington and Lincoln, we could prompt them with a thinking tool such as Ethics. When they create their graphic organizer, ask them to also sketch in the Ethics tool. Now they're comparing and contrasting the ethical issues that faced the two presidents. (Note that in this example, we're showing a different icon to represent Ethics in keeping with our idea that you can use whatever works for you.)

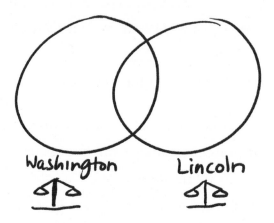

Compare and contrast is the Trends element, so you can definitely use Trends with a Venn. For example, let's say a social studies teacher is having students look at the Revolutionary War. She could ask students to evaluate the impact of the trend toward conflict in the Colonies. They could sketch out a Venn comparing the long-term causes with critical causes. Both types of causes would be Details, and the result is the Trend.

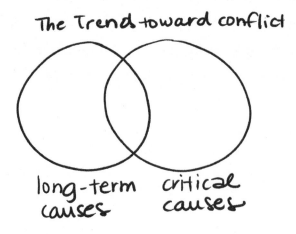

The students would sketch out their own Venn and label it with the Details icon. Some students could fill in the causes that were long-term, those that were critical, and those that were both. Other students could compare short-term causes and critical causes. Once they'd done this, they'd be ready to describe the Trend with a Big Idea. As we've mentioned before, it helps to scaffold that Big Idea so you get quality work, especially in the beginning. Here's a sample template a teacher could use:

The Big Idea of the Trend toward

conflict in the Colonies:

Critical issues such as ____ and _____ combined with the long-term issues of _____ and ____ resulted in an escalation of the conflict, eventually resulting in _____.

Math teachers could do the same thing with a self-reflection on students' challenges in different kinds of math problems. Students could consider the causes of difficulty when they first learned long division and compare that to the causes of difficulty they are currently experiencing with two-step, single variable problems (or any other combination).

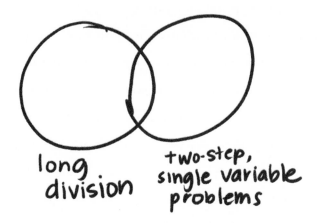

long division

two-step, single variable problems

After using a Venn diagram to compare the causes, they could then look at the Trend. Are there trends toward better comprehension, more frustration, less time required to learn, a need for more or fewer examples?

The scaffolded Big Idea could look something like this:

When I was learning long division, the causes of the difficulty I had were similar/different to those in learning two-step, single variable problems in that _____. Based on this, I believe the Trend in my math practice is toward greater/less need for practice before I learn a new idea.

Venns aren't limited to Trends, of course. Students could look closely at Details and combine that with Multiple Perspectives. How did the Colonists view the Revolutionary War compared to how the British saw it? How does the protagonist see the conflict compared to the way the antagonist sees it? How different is the experiment for two different compounds?

Venn diagrams can be used with any element of the framework:

- Compare the way we've seen this literary device used by two different authors. (Language of the Discipline and Details)
- Contrast the way the French and British monarchs handled demands for expanded freedoms. (Details)
- Compare the way the teacher sees lab safety to the way the students see lab safety. (Rules and Multiple Perspectives)
- Contrast the Sun to another star in the Milky Way galaxy. (Details)
- In a three-circle Venn diagram, represent these two ratios and percents with fractions, decimals, and concrete models. (Patterns, Language of the Discipline, and Rules)
- Compare and contrast the Patterns of Jupiter vs. Saturn.
- Compare and contrast how two species have Changed Over Time.

Other Possibilities

Any graphic organizer can be used with Depth and Complexity. There are lots of free ones available at the click of a button in Microsoft Office SmartArt – no need to venture into the wilds of the internet. All you have to do is click Insert – SmartArt, and a whole array of options will appear.

In this case, the teacher wants students to use a graphic organizer to sketch out the process by which a bill becomes a law.

The teacher chooses the Process choice on the left list of SmartArt options, and then choose the graphic that he/she likes best. The teacher then shows that one to the students as an example, and they sketch it out.

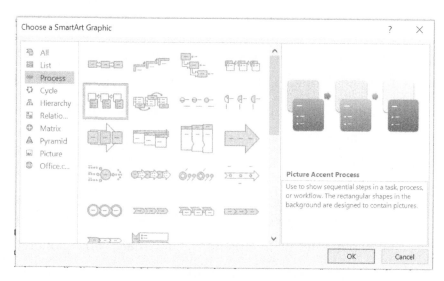

This simple graphic organizer is an alternative to a Venn diagram for showing the causes and effects of an event, idea, etc. I especially like breaking it into just the causes or just the effects so students can go deeper. Layering a prompt of depth and complexity onto this graphic organizer, we might look at the *rules*, *points of view*, and *changes* that caused the American Revolution.

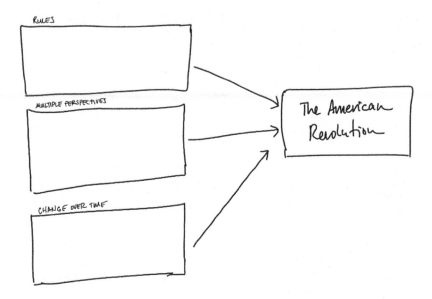

Or we could look at what *rules, points of view,* and *changes* resulted from the American Revolution.

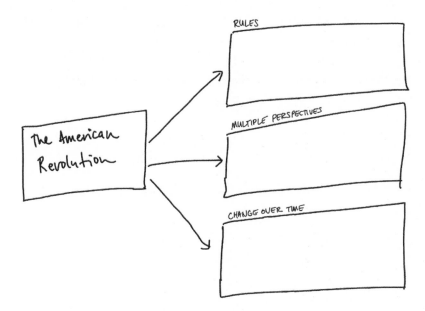

When working with negative numbers, what new *patterns* emerge in our calculations?

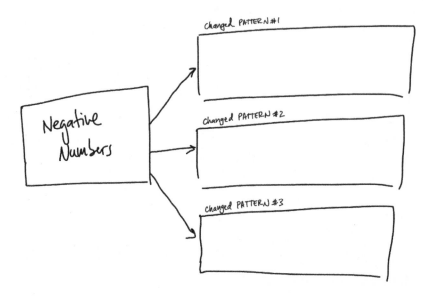

Other examples that could be used with this simple graphic organizer include:

- What changes over time led to Earth's moon? How has the moon led to new changes?
- What different points of view influenced Scout in *To Kill A Mockingbird*?
- What new rules did the Industrial Revolution lead to?

This SmartArt graphic organizer is a little more complex.

While it obviously would work for Change over Time, it's perfect for cycles. Think

- Nutrient cycle
- Oxygen cycle
- Phosphorus cycle
- Rock cycle
- Water cycle
- Moon cycle
- Seasons
- Rise and fall of civilizations

With SmartArt, you can add more sections with the (literal) click of a button, so you aren't limited by the default of three parts.

Some sample task statements include:

- Label this diagram with the three most complicated steps in the water cycle. Explain what makes each step complicated. (Details and Ethics)
- Label this diagram with the stages of the rock cycle. What would happen if the pattern broke and igneous rocks formed from erosion? Would we have more or fewer igneous rocks? (Patterns and Unanswered Questions)
- Use this diagram to illustrate a periodic sequence. (Patterns and Language of the Discipline)

While the internet is full of options for graphic organizers, we like SmartArt to get ideas because it's free and, if your students are creating them digitally, they can adjust the colors and insert text as well as add and subtract sections.

Thing Maps® and Depth and Complexity

If Thinking Maps® had a Facebook page, their status would say, "In a long-term, committed relationship with Depth & Complexity." Seriously, they are a match made in pedagogy heaven. Thinking Maps (thinkingmaps.com) and Depth & Complexity are a very natural fit. In our opinion, Thinking Maps in conjunction with the Depth & Complexity model and Bloom's taxonomy provide a complete structure for supporting higher-order thinking.

If you're not familiar with the Thinking Maps model, it is "a language of eight visual patterns each based on a fundamental thinking process. These patterns are used individually and in combination across every grade level and curriculum area as an integrated set of tools for life-long learning" (*A Language for Learning*, 2). While they look like graphic organizers, they're far deeper.

We believe that the most important goal of teaching is to prepare our students to be autodidacts, able to teach themselves over a lifetime. Individual content in isolation has limited value in the long-term. The models of Depth & Complexity and Thinking Maps are powerful tools for the creation and support of solid thinkers. That common goal means they are excellent partners.

24

USING FRAMES

THE DEPTH AND COMPLEXITY FRAMEWORK asks students to stay with an idea longer, examining it from multiple perspective, exploring connections to other topics, and teasing out the pros and cons. The frame graphic organizer is a perfect complement to this process.

A frame looks like a picture frame. In the middle goes the topic and then each of the four sides is an opportunity to delve into that topic in a different way. A frame doesn't have to follow a linear order like a table would imply. Each of the four sides can build on each other or they can be completely separate. The key is to make certain that any Frame you use is truly pushing students towards deeper and more complex thinking.

Frames typically come in one of two variations. The first one is composed of four trapezoids surrounding a rectangle.

You can turn the frame to a portrait orientation or use it in landscape orientation (shown below). As indicated, that center box can be adjusted in size, and this will adjust the size of the trapezoids, too.

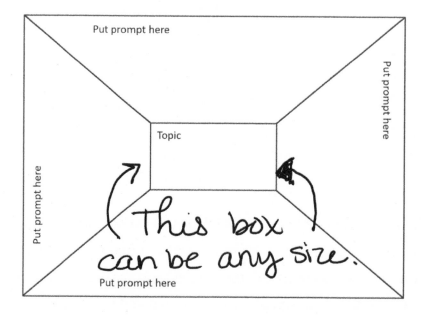

The second kind of frame you'll see has designated space for the prompts in the corners, rectangular spaces next to them, and then a rectangle in the middle for illustrations, more content, etc.

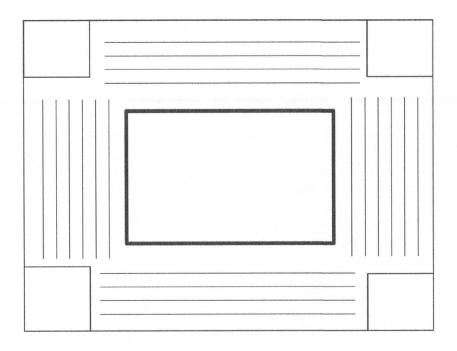

How People Get Frames Wrong

The biggest mistake we see people do with frames is to focus on "using a frame" but not considering whether the frame pushes students to think in a new way. They plop an icon all by itself in each of the four sections. A student will see, for example, Details in the top. Then there's a Rules icon, a Patterns icon, and a Big Idea. But without clear direction, each of those sections just becomes a list. If it's just a Details icon, students will default to listing details. That's the bottom of Bloom's. Kids rush through since it's so simple.

Instead, each section of a frame should stop students in their tracks. It should make them put their pencil down and think. Write out a question in each section using a complete sentence (or even multiple sentences!). Consider how each prompt will offer a more complex view of the topic in the middle.

They Need an Example

There are two common problems with examples. The first is when a teacher gives no example at all. The second problem is when we give an example that is over the top.

First, no example is not okay. We need models to set expectations. Without them, perfectionists will obsess that they *haven't done enough* while unmotivated students give what Lisa's Grandma called "a lick and a promise." We all work best from an exemplar, so give one.

The other mistake we see is when teachers creates an example that looks like someone with an advanced degree in curriculum and instruction made. There's nothing left for a student to do without copying the teacher's work.

One suggestion for good practice is to create a frame for a similar, though not identical, topic. For instance, a language arts teacher could work through a frame about a similar story (a different Dr. Seuss story, for example). In math, maybe you'd have students complete a frame about the Distributive Property, but you could model the same thing for the Associative Property.

Modeling is essential to guide students to where we want to go. Just be careful that the model doesn't give everything away!

What's Its Why?

In order for your frame to be effective, you need to be clear about what you're asking it to do. Is your purpose to:

- Focus more closely on one aspect of a piece of content?
- Differentiate instruction?
- Encourage students to unpack their thinking?
- Replace a quiz or other less engaging assignment?
- Allow for interest-driven engagement in the content?
- Encourage integration of a graphic or image?

Choose your purpose so that your final outcome aligns with what you were hoping for. Without the purpose, you may find yourself feeling vaguely dissatisfied that the students didn't produce what you were hoping for. Let's look closely at each of these scenarios.

Do You Want to Focus on One Aspect of Your Content?

Want to focus closely on just one piece of content? Then, consider the ways in which students get that content wrong and how you can use Depth and Complexity to clarify it.

For example, if your students are frequently confusing vocabulary, then you can include Language of the Discipline questions specifically designed to focus on often-misunderstood words.

There's no rule that you can you have to have four different elements in a frame. It's perfectly fine to have the same element repeated in the frame. If Language of the Discipline is what your students need, then feel free to ask about it in more than one section of the Frame.

To focus more closely on a piece of content, ask questions that require deep thinking. Get specific! These questions should require students to get their hands dirty. Here are examples:

- Why do you think the word ____ gets confused with the word ____? (Language of the Discipline)
- Think of a way someone could make sure they never get those two words confused. (Language of the Discipline)
- In what way is this most closely related to ____ and why is that relationship important? (Patterns)
- Think of three key rules this ____ must follow and how they are most often broken. (Rules)
- In what way is the way that this looks when you first see it different from the way it looks after you've thought about it awhile? (Multiple Perspectives)

Do you see the level of focus required in each of these questions? If you ask broad questions, you will not get specific results you're looking for in this scenario.

Do You Want to Differentiate Instruction?

Differentiation is one the key uses of Frames. You can do it (at least) three ways:

- Have students work in a group using the same Frame

- Have students respond to different questions related to the same content

- Have students work on different content with the same questions

Let's look at each of these ideas one at a time.

First, how do you have students work in a group in the same frame? It's pretty straightforward and non-techy. Literally cut the frame apart, giving each student a section (or two). You can even include the middle of the frame as its own section that a student can complete. When they've each finished their part, have them glue their pieces onto an intact frame. You may wish to put the frame on a legal-sized piece of paper for this one to allow for more space.

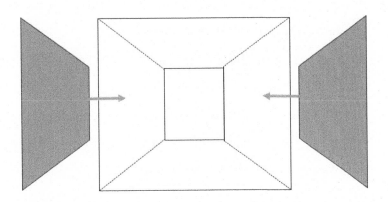

The other two scenarios are straightforward. You can differentiate the task questions, or you can differentiate the content itself. Here's an example of differentiating task statements. Let's say your students are working on a frame about even numbers. Your highest-level learners would have task questions like this:

- Zero does not have a Roman numeral. Invent one. (Language of the Discipline)
- What is another valuable name we could call the set of even numbers? (Language of the Discipline)
- Which is friendlier, the set of even numbers or the set of odd numbers? (Across Disciplines)
- If you add an even number and an odd number, the sum will be an odd number. Does that mean that odd numbers are stronger than even numbers? (Multiple Perspectives)

Your on-level learners would also be working with even numbers, but their questions would be adjusted as follows:

- What happens if you add two even numbers? Do you get an even number or an odd number? (Details)
- What are the benefits of being able to separate numbers into even and odd? (Ethics)
- Do you think it's right that zero is an even number? (Ethics)
- What do you know about even numbers that you didn't know last year? (Change over Time)

Your learners who need more support would also be working with even numbers, but their questions would be adjusted as follows:

- What are numbers you could add to the number 7 to make an even number? Choose three. (Details)

- How could you tell someone how to tell if a number is even? (Details)
- What is your favorite even number and why? (Unanswered Questions)
- If you subtract 3 from 10, do you get an even number or an odd number? Make up two problems, one that results in an odd number, and one that results in an even number. (Details)

They're all doing the same activity, but the level of thinking is significantly different.

The last option is perhaps the most simple of all. Change the content your students are working with. If one group is doing even numbers, let another group do integers. If one group is analyzing a cinquain poem, another group could be analyzing a more complex poetic structure, like a sonnet. If one group is considering the causes of World War II, the other group could be comparing those causes to those of a previous conflict.

One thing that can go wrong here is when teachers confuse length for complexity. For example, if some students are working with the Preamble to the Constitution while others are examining the Gettysburg Address, the Gettysburg text may seem more challenging because it's longer. However, the Preamble addresses thousands of years of political philosophy, while Gettysburg is finite in scope, making it much easier to analyze. Don't make the *more*-ferentiation mistake! Just because it's longer doesn't make it "thinkier." We just made up that word.

Do You Want to Encourage Students to Unpack Their Thinking?

Sometimes you may wish to use a frame to help students justify their thinking. Lots of assignments tell students to "justify your answer" or "show your work." That can be a lot like telling a six-year-old to clean his room. They need it broken down, step-by-step. You can do this with a frame.

For math, consider putting the problem in the center of the frame. Then, in each section, have the students look at the problem through different lenses of the framework. Here's an example:

- In the center of the frame is this story/word problem: Mateo is having a birthday party. He has fifteen cupcakes. How many people can he invite to his party so that everyone can have two cupcakes?

- In one section, focus on Language of the Discipline: What words would a mathematician use to describe this problem? Can you come up with four?

- In another section, use Ethics to ask: What should Mateo's dad tell him if he wants to invite an extra person, but there aren't enough cupcakes for that person?

- In another section, show a Multiple Perspectives icon and ask: If you were the cupcakes, would you rather have one of you eaten by lots of kids or two of you eaten by fewer kids?

- In the last section, combine Patterns and Rules to ask: Solve Mateo's issue, applying the Patterns and Rules you've learned about this type of problem.

We can do the same for language arts when students are asked to use evidence from the text. Rather than just have them go grab a sentence fragment or highlight a word or two, set up a frame that helps them analyze the content. Imagine the question is something like, "What did the author do to create suspense in the story?" You could put questions around the frame such as:

- Which part of the story did the question make you think of first? (Details)
- If someone said that you had to prove that the author *didn't* use suspense, would that be harder or easier than showing how she did? (Unanswered Questions)
- Which other story can you think of that you could also use to support the answer to this question? What other story's author used suspense? (Across Disciplines)
- Using a sentence with at least three words from the story in it in quotes, share what you think is the strongest response to this question. (Details)

In the center, share a Big Idea icon and put in a template such as: Authors use _____ and _____, and sometimes _____ to create suspense on the part of the reader.

Do You Want to Replace A Quiz or Other
Less-Engaging Assignment?

Quizzes are necessary and good, but they don't always have to be in the same format. You can use a frame to obtain the same information about the students' mastery of the topic without multiple choice questions. For example, Lisa's quiz on the Blue Whale has not a multiple-choice question to be seen, yet she can easily assess students' level of comprehension and application in their understanding of her favorite animal.

To use a frame as a quiz, simply choose the elements you want, and put the icons you are using in the corners of the frame. Display a master on the screen or document camera with the questions on the frame, as shown in Lisa's quiz below. Note that on the display, she puts the bottom task question right side up, even though students will answer with the text upside down because they will have turned their paper. Putting the task question right side up makes it easier for students to read.

In this example, Lisa's got the following:

- A Patterns question (What would happen if you moved the Blue Whale up one level in the food web?)

- A Multiple Perspectives question (What land animal is most like the Blue Whale in size *and* personality?)

- An Ethics question (Why is it a good idea or not for one animal to be so much larger than the other animals in the ocean?)

- An Across Disciplines question (What is a Blue Whale's favorite number and why?)

There is no way for a student to respond reasonably without a solid knowledge of the Blue Whale. Bonus: these are much more fun to grade than a regular quiz!

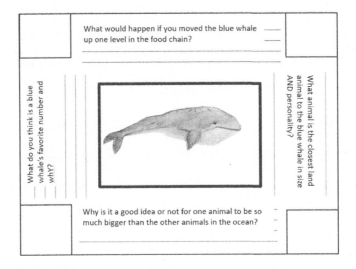

Allow for Interest-driven Engagement in the Content?

Differentiation can be done for interest as well as ability, so feel free to use frames to allow students to explore their interests. You can gauge student interests with a frame of entirely Unanswered Questions, such as:

- If you could go anywhere in the world, where would you go and what would you most like to see?
- If you could do over one week of school, which week would it be and why?

- Which book do you think other people really like that you don't really like?
- Why do you think you might be Ms. So-and-So's secret favorite student (even though she doesn't have favorites)?

The possibilities for this are endless. Of course, you can use it for actual content, too. What did students think was hardest? What did they like best? What was most similar to what they'd heard before? What would they have liked to spend more or less time on? Get a peek into your students' minds with frames!

Do You Want to Encourage Integration of a Graphic or Image?

With a frame, you can combine images and written content. Students can create a visual in the center (use dot-to-dot outlines if you want to guide younger students). They can then use the outer sections for related information.

Ask students to create a graphic (a map, a coordinate plane, etc.) in the middle and then fill the frame with their own questions. Then, they can trade with another student and answer each others' questions.

Many grade-levels ask students to interpret images and graphs. You can also use frames to practice this skill. Put a map projection in the middle and ask questions like:

- What is the name of this map projection? (Language of the Discipline)
- Who would be most likely to use this projection? Least likely? (Multiple Perspectives)

- Who used this map projection first? (Unanswered Question if not previously discussed; Details if previously discussed)

- Of all of the map projections you know, where does this one rank in terms of how badly it misshapes Greenland? (Ethics)

Put a graph showing car sales in the center and ask questions such as:

- Based on this graph, which day do you think you would want to work at the car dealership if you made money based on how many cars were sold? (Unanswered Questions)

- Who buys more cars, people who like big cars or people who like small cars? (Details)

- Why do you think more people buy cars on weekends than on weekdays? (Unanswered Questions)

- Based on this graph, how many cars do you think will be sold next Monday? (Patterns)

There's something about putting the graph in the center and letting kids spin the paper around as they respond that makes it more engaging. Perhaps it's the kinesthetics of it or perhaps it's the fact that the teacher needs to create better task questions! Whatever the reason, it's effective.

Don't Be a Lister!

Whether you use some of our examples or break out on your own, as long as you avoid the curse of the blank frame, you'll be fine. The blank frame is the one we mentioned at the beginning of the chapter – you know, the one with icons splashed on it and nothing else? Yeah, that one. Don't do that.

You can see from the example task questions we shared that there's a lot more to be done with frames than to ask students to just list the Ethics, list the Rules, list the Patterns, etc. No listiness! Don't be a lister! Embrace the power of frames by encouraging deep thinking through great questions in your frames.

25

COMBINING THE ELEMENTS

IF THE DEPTH AND COMPLEXITY ELEMENTS were to receive a report card, under the citizenship section it would receive an "outstanding" for "Plays well with others." Each element practically begs to be combined with other elements, so let's dive into some of the possible combinations. Keep in mind that due to the nature of combinations, you're going to see the elements repeated. For example, if we combine Details with Big Idea, you will likely see that combo suggested under both Details and Big Idea.

Details

Details is perhaps the most agreeable of all the elements. There is not a single element it does not combine with easily. That can cause its own issues, though, because you may find yourself leaning on it too heavily to the exclusion of other prompts.

Details pairs nicely with Big Idea because you need Details to support the Big Idea. (We dive deeply into that in Chapter 4.) These two are such a natural fit that this is the first pair of elements Ian introduces to students.

Patterns also is a great element to combine with Details because Details form Patterns. You can't recognize a Pattern if you can't identify the key Details.

We also recommend Language of the Discipline as a possible strong combination pair. Often, the key to understanding a math problem lies in recognizing which words in the problem are vital (Details) and what those words mean (Language of the Discipline).

Details plus Ethics often lead to Unanswered Questions. This is a great reminder that we shouldn't limit ourselves to just two elements when considering possible combinations.

Big Idea

As we've already mentioned, Big Idea and Details are a natural fit. Here are three introductory ideas for incorporating Big Ideas and Details into a task:

1. Ask students to identify an *interesting* Big Idea and then support it with at least four essential Details. Push them when their Big Ideas are not sufficiently interesting.

2. Offer students several possible Big Ideas about a topic and ask each child to choose one Big Idea to support with

Details. Remember, if you offer the Big Idea, it should be slightly beyond students' natural reach.

3. Connect beyond one topic, asking students to create a Big Idea that applies to several stories, people, events, or other topics, using Detail to explain how the story, person, event, or topic supports the unifying Big Idea.

There are many more ways to integrate Big Idea and Details, so as you try these out, more ideas will come to you.

In addition to Details, Big Idea combines nicely with Across Disciplines. This is partly because Across Disciplines begs for a Big Idea: Why are these things appropriate for connection? If I ask my geometry students to analyze a map through the lens of geometry, finding particular shapes or angles on a topographical map, it is very useful to then ask them to evaluate the strength and validity of the exercise itself. Why is this a useful exercise? What can we say about the connection between geometry and cartography (specifically) or geography (more generally)?

We also like to combine Big Idea with Patterns. You learned more fully in Chapter 7 that Patterns are things that repeat or cycle, things that have a recurring element. Consider plot in a story. Plot is pattern. We have an inciting incident, followed by rising action, then a climax, then falling action and resolution. We also see Pattern in literary archetypes like the villain, the hero, etc. Consider how this can combine with Big Idea. Questions that require students to evaluate the theme (Big Idea) of a story against Pattern (plot, archetype) lead to deeper thinking about both elements of the story. I can lead rich discussions with questions such as, "In the story, the major theme we discussed was the Big Idea that the value of friendship is greater when you didn't have any friends before. Who proved that better, the hero or the villain?"

Lastly, Multiple Perspectives serves two roles with Big Idea. First, when students are constructing a quality Big Idea, they often need to see the object of their analysis from more than one aspect or perspective. Secondly, if students generate a less-than-stellar Big Idea, we may need to gently direct them to Multiple Perspectives to help them see the broader picture. Crafting a quality Big Idea is tricky when attempted through only one lens. If we're looking at the Big Idea of a sphere, we do that best in three dimensions, not two. The same is true of less literal examples. I can't really analyze an event in history if viewed from only one side of a conflict (Well, I *can*, but it won't be a very good analysis!).

- A Big Idea can Change over Time
- Perspectives affect the identification of a Big Idea
- There are often ethical implications to a Big Idea
- New information/details will force us to revise a Big Idea

Language of the Discipline

The best friends of Language of the Discipline are Details, Patterns, and Rules. In many ways, Language of the Discipline could be considered a subset of Details. It is part of what makes any domain different, unique, and special. It is a signifier, a distinguisher. Students can evaluate which words are most important, which tools/skills are most difficult/necessary to use, or even create new acronyms for sets of words. We often frequently ask students to highlight or notate the words that are essential to solving a problem or analyzing a text. This is a Language of the Discipline activity.

The words themselves often have patterns, so Patterns fits beautifully. Identifying the common roots, prefixes, and suffixes in a word can help students figure out the meanings of related words. Consider the connection between "interval" and "integer." Understanding that "inter" means "between" can help otherwise unfamiliar words feel much more approachable.

Words themselves often follow rules, so Rules is another great match for Language of the Discipline. We're used to hearing "Remember, 'I' before 'E' except after 'C' / and when it spells 'A' as in 'neighbor' and 'way'." There are other rules, too, that involve Language of the Discipline. There are Rules for what makes a right triangle, what makes a coordinating conjunction necessary, how many of what type of note will fit in a measure, and on and on.

Rules

We'll discuss how Rules and Patterns are a natural fit in the next section, and Rules has other friends among the elements as well. Ethics makes an interesting partner element as students analyze the fairness of rules or how the breaking of a rule may be justified. A favorite essay topic in Lisa's English class asks, "In *The*

Scarlet Letter, are the rules society imposes on women fair? How does it punish the breaking of those rules? Who else is punished besides the rule-breaker and how?" Her advanced students answer a slightly different, but still rules-based prompt: "Compare the rules society imposes on women in *The Scarlet Letter* and argue either that the rules have changed, or the punishments are more subtle."

The argument could be made that in many content areas it is impossible to examine the Rules without Ethics. This isn't just true for people or characters because we can raise thinking level by anthropomorphizing inanimate objects. Is it fair that producers in the food chain are always at the bottom? How are producers like house elves in *Harry Potter*? How do the Rules benefit some people and harm others? Latitude and Longitude are Rules because if you don't follow them, you get lost. Is it fair that the whole Earth is gridded from this one tiny place in England? Where would be a fairer place to locate the prime meridian? Is there one?

We can look at Rules with Multiple Perspectives as well. Explain the rules of baseball from the perspective of the ball. Explain the rules of lab safety from the perspective of the lab itself. Keeping in mind that organization is part of Rules, we can look at the way certain people, things, or interest groups are benefitted or hindered by organizational structures. Who benefits most from the idea that the Northern Hemisphere is "up"? Showing a map with the hemispheres switched from their typical layout on a globe is sure to cause some discussion.

Patterns

Like most Depth and Complexity elements, Patterns plays well with others. You've already read a fairly lengthy analysis of how it plays with Rules, and we like it with a couple of others as well. Ethics complements Patterns well because in Ethics we are often confronted with fairness and our perception of what is fair is often influenced by patterns of behavior.

Like Details, Patterns can also be used to support Big Ideas or even other Patterns. In what way does the Pattern of the rise and fall of civilizations mimic the rock cycle? If students are given the Big Idea, "Everything is a remix," or "Everything old is new again," they can use Patterns to support that.

Patterns pairs well with Multiple Perspectives in some instances. Does everyone see this Pattern the same way? For instance, does plankton think about the food web in the same way the blue whale does? (There is no way Lisa could go through a whole book on curriculum and instruction without a blue whale reference!). Does the Pattern support or argue against a character's viewpoint? Does everyone benefit equally from the Pattern? Who would benefit most if it were broken?

Combining Patterns with Rules is particularly interesting. One of Ian's favorite Depth moves is to ask students to find the patterns in a situation, and then ask how those patterns have (or might) lead to new rules. But you can also reverse this move by asking students to first look for rules, and then think about how those rules might (or did) create new patterns.

Unanswered Questions

Because resources change in their availability, we frequently combine Change over Time with Unanswered Questions. What did we used to think about this versus what we think now? What might we still learn in the future? What would have happened if this character had lived at a different time/place? Even something as straightforward as asking students to consider what they thought they knew about a piece of content but turned out not to be correct combines Change over Time with Unanswered Questions. The place we occupy in time greatly impacts the Unanswered Questions we have, so these two elements will be common companions in your classroom.

Details combines well, too, because often need to parse out the Details to determine what still remains to be answered. If we're too casual with the Details, we end up with weak Unanswered Questions. We see that when students don't pay attention to instructions being given and then ask questions that were just answered (That's not a phenomenon limited to students!). We see it even more when we don't carefully examine the Details and so believe something is an Unanswered Question when it is not, or we have the incorrect Unanswered Question.

Perhaps the most rewarding element to combine with Unanswered Questions is Ethics. Ethics just makes everything better, and that's true of this element as well. Putting these two powerhouses together leads to great thinking. It doesn't have to be a huge existential question, either. Consider this question asked of fifth graders about the Corps of Discovery (the Lewis and Clark expedition): Is it fair to consider Lewis a failure for not finding something that did not exist?

This is an example of how simple differentiation becomes with Depth and Complexity. That question is one the highest level students answered, while the on-level students responded to the less rigorous task, "Compare the unanswered questions that guided Lewis and Clark with those that guided another explorer." Students who needed even more scaffolding responded to this prompt: "What were the Unanswered Questions that guided the Corps of Discovery?"

Claire Hughes, a professor at the College of Coastal Georgia, explains that when we are tiering instruction, we use this framework: all will...most should...some could. The lowest students will accomplish what all must know, the on-level students will explore what would be good to know, and the highest level learners will often be able to reach into what is also interesting to know. With Depth and Complexity, this becomes second nature as we get stronger at asking questions with varying levels of mental challenge.

We talk about the importance of understanding that differentiation is not as much about what students are doing as much as it is about what they are thinking. When we combine elements as strong as Ethics and Unanswered Questions, we can raise the thinking levels of our students without having them engage in a completely different activity.

Trends

Use Trends with Over Time to examine if there is a time component to the Trend. You can analyze if the forces acting on the Trend are different than they would have been in a different time period.

Details have to be identified if we're going to clearly evaluate a Trend, and often we'll look at Details to see if there is a Trend. Factors are a part of Details, so they will be what supports the Trend in the same way they support Big Idea.

Another element that works well with Trends is Ethics. Remember that Ethics looks at pros and cons, so that's a good fit for whether the direction something is heading is positive or negative. A wonderful technique is to analyze the pros and cons of the forces themselves, and then look at the pros and cons of the effects and see if there is alignment or discrepancy. Just as things get interesting when Patterns break, things get really complicated when the forces are positives, but the Trends are negative or vice versa.

Ethics

We like to introduce Ethics with Multiple Perspectives because to really understand an ethical issue it helps to see that problem from a different view of the problem. You may wish to consider that beautiful fit when you're planning on how you're going to introduce the elements.

That said, Ethics is perhaps the equal opportunity element: it works with almost everything.

Consider that:

- Ethical issues often lead to new Rules.
- Rules sometimes lead to new ethical issues.
- Change leads to ethical issues.
- Different points of view see ethical issues differently.
- Rules both solve and create ethical problems.

In order to be accurate in an evaluation of Ethics, the Details have to be clear and agreed upon. If we differ in what we think the facts are, we will have more trouble discussing more complex issues accurately and appropriately.

Change over Time

You can march this element across a broad spectrum of its siblings. Rather than just asking how TVs have changed over time, prompt students to think about how the Rules about TVs have changed, how have the specific Details on TVs changed, how have the Ethics surrounding TVs changed? What are the Trends we've noticed in TV over Time?

It combines especially well with Patterns because Patterns are themselves somewhat time dependent. We see this in things like the water cycle, the rock cycle, and the plot of stories. In history, this combination will be common.

Details support the identification of the Change over Time. What were the specifics before compared to what they were afterwards?

Language of the Discipline fits in here, too, because sometimes the nomenclature changes. For instance, Mt. Denali used to be called Mt. McKinley. Sometimes countries change their names (some change them and then back again, like the Congo, I mean Zaire, I mean Congo).

Words like "cloud" and "tablet" mean something very different now than they did fifteen years ago, and there are examples of this in every domain. Are they "story problems" or "word problems"?

Across Disciplines

Across Disciplines plays well with the Patterns element. It's partly the recognition of patterns that enables us to make connections. For example, in what ways does the rock cycle mimic the rise and fall of civilizations? In order to examine that, we need to use the Patterns in both the rock cycle and the civilization rise/fall cycle. Oftentimes, the connections they make in seeing how something they've learned previously can be applied to what they're learning now is a result of seeing a similarity of Patterns.

Across Disciplines also works well with the Trends element. This is handy – two underappreciated elements working together! Because Trends looks at the direction something is moving or changing, it allows students to say, "This is how this was the last time we saw it (Across Disciplines), and it's changed in this way because of this thing" (Trends).

Lastly, Multiple Perspectives is a great fit because sometimes the reason we're making a connection is because we're seeing something from a different point of view. We're noticing a connection or making a thought bridge because we are looking at it from the perspective of someone with more experience or from a different content area. Ask students, "When you saw problems like this before, you used this technique to solve them. Now, from the perspective of a 5th grader instead of a 3rd grader, how would you solve it?"

Multiple Perspectives

Multiple Perspectives and Ethics are in a long-term, very committed relationship. Both elements deal with the idea of bias and both depend on one's viewpoint. Even whether we see something as an ethical issue or not is partly dependent upon our perspective. Often, the way you perceive an Ethics issue has everything to do with how invested you are in a situation.

Because Change over Time so often leads to new perspectives, we have to make sure to pair these elements. What did people think of an idea hundreds of years ago versus now? How will we see this in the future? Is the ocean happier than it was two thousand years ago?

Multiple Perspectives are not fully knowable. We can make reasonable guesses, but we'll never really know. That makes it the perfect element to pair with Unanswered Questions. There's inherent mystery in both elements.

Similarly, we use Patterns to make educated guesses about Multiple Perspectives. Part of how I examine Multiple Perspectives is by looking at past Patterns.

Wrapping Up

Hopefully this chapter has provided you with some jumping off points for combining elements. It's important to keep in mind that none of these ideas should be seen as limiting. These are possible ideas, not prescriptive ideas. You can – and should – combine the elements in any way you like. There are no elements that are like bleach and ammonia (don't mix them!). Nothing will blow up if you combine elements in ways we did not suggest, so combine away.

26

PLANNING WITH DEPTH AND COMPLEXITY

ONE OF OUR PURPOSES in writing this book was to help teachers feel like they knew how to get started with the framework. A friend of Lisa's mentioned to her that he used Depth and Complexity to plan, and she asked if he'd write up an explanation of how he did it. He agreed, and so this chapter is a little us and a lot of him. In addition to being Lisa's friend, Andrew McBurney is an AP Government teacher and Social Studies Department Chair at a high school in San Antonio, Texas.

Planning with Depth and Complexity: What It Must Do

Your planning needs to result in your using Depth and Complexity in a way that works for you and is aligned with the requirements you have. We all have standards and objectives we're working with, and our districts may also want us to use other systems or programs. We have to have a way to blend all of together that doesn't make us feel overwhelmed.

How Andrew Does Depth and Complexity

I had been incorporating dimensions of Depth and Complexity into some of my lessons for a few weeks, when I decided that I needed to plan for them more methodically. I found myself falling into a rut of using the same kinds of activities to hit dimensions like Language of the Discipline (vocabulary activities), Trends (draw conclusions from points plotted on a graph), or Multiple Perspectives (current events discussions).

Additionally, I was using these activities more or less as they occurred to me as I was preparing for my lessons. I was going through the school year, as I usually do, "tweaking" my existing lessons—this time, by "ramping up" a few activities here and there, or adding a few new ones, that made use of the dimensions of Depth and Complexity.

I knew I wasn't doing as good a job as I could be with Depth and Complexity, so I identified my needs:

1) I needed to put more thought into the activities I was using, and really ask myself if I was staying true to the intent of the dimensions I was using; and

2) I needed a better plan for using the dimensions of Depth and Complexity, so that I wasn't using them like sprinkles on an ice cream cone.

Then I needed a starting point. I decided that since I was just starting out, I wasn't going to try to rework all my lessons in one fell swoop. I started with one lesson in particular. It wasn't the lesson that needed the most work—it was a good lesson that I felt had the potential to be better. If I was going to do this, I wanted a lesson that had the potential to show what Depth and Complexity could really achieve.

Make a Chart

I took one of those Depth and Complexity charts—the kind that shows the elements of depth on the vertical axis, and the elements of complexity on the horizontal axis—and recreated it on a larger piece of paper. Then I took my lesson and wrote the objectives at the top, outside of the chart itself. Then, I wrote out all of the activities where they would fit in the chart. This is an essential step because it tells you 1) what you are already doing that fits elements of Depth and Complexity; 2) what you are already doing that doesn't actually fit very well into any of the elements of Depth and Complexity (I wrote these out to the side); and 3) allows you to see what squares are left blank—in other words, the gaps.

Let me say something about those gaps. First, it may be that some gaps are fine. I want to be clear that I am not suggesting that every lesson reflect every combination of the elements of Depth and Complexity. There are some activities that you could do with your lesson that may not actually be relevant to your objectives. It's okay to leave some of the squares blank.

However, a look at those empty squares may indicate to you things you should be doing, but aren't. Spend some time on those squares and think of what you could add.

Review the Activities

Next, go back and review the squares you had initially filled with activities. Check yourself—Does each activity line up with your objectives? Is there anything you should do to refine the activity so that it better aligns with your objectives?

Then review the activities that didn't fit, that you wrote out to the side. Are any of them essential as basic, foundational activities? Could they fit with other activities in the chart? Can any of them be discarded?

Starting from Scratch

So, I started from scratch—or, rather, I tried to anyway. I really started a handful of lessons from scratch. I picked the lessons I felt would lend themselves most obviously to using dimensions of Depth and Complexity and started there. (The truth is, by the way, that the more you work with Depth and Complexity, the more you realize that every lesson lends itself to Depth and Complexity. In fact, at this point, I would say, if you feel you have a lesson where Depth and Complexity doesn't really apply, then you aren't doing it right.)

I laid out the state standards for the lessons, Bloom's Taxonomy, Webb's Depth of Knowledge, and the dimensions of

Depth and Complexity. I also had at hand the resources I knew I would utilize, including the textbook and additional sources.

The Chart

Unit: _____

Lesson: _____

	Across the Disciplines Where else do we see it?	Change over Time How is it/was it/will it be?	Multiple Perspectives Who or what sees it differently?
Details Just the facts.			
Patterns Details combined into relationships.			
Trends Details combined into directions (temporal relationships).			
Rules Details combined into ordering principles (hierarchical relationships).			
Big Ideas Concepts and theories.			
Ethics Moral principles and controversies.			
Unanswered Questions "Here be dragons."			
Language of the Discipline			

Note: We have a full-sized version of the chart you can download at giftedguild.com/dcextras.

What We Love about Andrew's Ideas

- We love that he is so intentional about having a process. Not knowing how to start is what stymies so many of us. This method gives teachers a concrete path. Here, fill this in.

- Encouraging teachers to focus on objectives and activities helps make sure the lesson is aligned and engaging, which is super helpful.

- The subdivisions between the elements give some visual space in the chart.

- Having Language of the Discipline laid out across the bottom makes it easy to identify and focus on the academic vocabulary associated with each lesson.

- Those little descriptors in the box with each element are helpful, especially for teachers new to the framework. "Here be dragons" is our favorite!

Implementing Andrew's Method

Here are some key takeaways from Andrew's method that we think lots of teachers can use:

- Start with a single lesson rather than trying to revise an entire unit or semester at a time. Slow and steady...

- Be intentional. Stay focused on what you're trying to accomplish and the ways in which Depth and Complexity can help you do that.

- Stay true to the standards. Andrew's method shows how you can use Depth and Complexity to make sure you're hitting your standards effectively. It's not just checking them off; it's really analyzing the lesson to consider what kind of thinking you're using and if that thinking is the best kind of thinking for the standard.

- Use a chart or visual to help you see all of the pieces. We've mentioned that you don't want to march some piece of content through all of the lens of the framework, but a chart will help you see if you're consistently using the same ones over and over when you could benefit from expanding your element universe a little bit. It also helps you stay true to the other standards you're using (he mentioned DOK, Bloom's, etc.).

Where You Go from Here

We're not saying you have to use Andrew's method. What we hope you glean from this chapter is the idea that when you are starting out, it helps to have a plan. It helps to consider your needs and goals and how Depth and Complexity can help you meet those goals.

We hope you can use the chart (or an adaptation of it). We hope you can use his sharing of his process to discover a process that works for you.

27

CONCLUSION

THE PRIMARY AIM OF THIS BOOK is to provide a guide for any teacher wanting to implement Depth and Complexity into the classroom. Our intention was to show you a path to follow that will allow you to raise your students' thinking. We hope we've done that.

Mostly, we hope that you will feel confident venturing into the world of Depth and Complexity, already knowing the most common pitfalls to avoid. Even if none of the specific activities or ideas apply directly to your content, we hope that you have been persuaded that you can use the Framework and that it has a place in your classroom.

The Big Idea of this book is that Depth and Complexity is for everyone, and a few simple *this, not that* adjustments make it approachable for teachers in every content area and grade level. The Unanswered Question is whether you will try it. Will you give it a shot? Will you look at how it can help you and venture out into the world of Depth and Complexity? We hope so, and we hope to guide you as you explore this powerful tool.

APPENDIX

APPENDIX A:

POSSIBLE PRODUCTS

add a chapter to a book

announcements

autobiographies

ballads

brochures

booklets

bumper stickers

cartoon or comic

chart

children's book

commentaries

data table

demonstrations

dialogues

dictionaries

directions

drawings or illustrations

event chains

explanations

fact sheets

flag

folk tales

games / puzzles

graffiti

graphic organizer

historical (I was there...)

inventions

advertisements

audio

awards

billboards

book jackets

bulletin board

captions

case study

cereal boxes

collage

conversations

definitions

designs

diary entries

dioramas or displays

drama scripts

editorials or essays

experiments

fables or fairy tales

family tree

flow chart

friendly letter

game boards

graph

guidebooks

interviews

invitations

jokes

jump rope jingles

legends

lies

lyrics

manuals

memoirs

models

murals

music video

newscasts

obituaries

peer editing

photo album

poems

postcards

presentations

puppet shows

recipe

research report

resumes

rules of etiquette

scenery for play

scrapbook

shadow box

signs or sketches

songs

story problem

survey

timeline

weather map

written debates

journals

labels

letters

lists

magazine page

maps

menus

movie scripts

museum display

myths

newspaper articles

pamphlets

petition

plays

position statements

poster

proposals

reader's theatre

requests

responses to literature

reviews of books

scale models

science display

sculpture

short story

skits

speeches

summaries

time capsule

tribute

wishes

Appendix B:

References

California Association for the Gifted (1994). Differentiating the core curriculum and instruction to provide advanced learning opportunities. Sacramento, CA: California State Dept. of Education. Retrieved from ERIC database. (ED375598)

DiCecco, V. M., & Gleason, M. M. (2002). *Using graphic organizers to attain relational knowledge from expository text.* Journal of Learning Disabilities, 35, 306–320.

Hyerle, D. & Yeager, C. (2007). *Thinking Maps: A Language for Learning.*

Kim, A., Vaughn, S., Wanzek, J., & Wei, S. (2004). *Graphic organizers and their effects on the reading comprehension of students with LD: A synthesis of research.* Journal of Learning Disabilities, 37, 105–118.

Lipton, L., & Wellman, B. (1998). *Patterns and practices in the learning-focused classroom.* Guilford, Vermont: Pathways Publishing.

Manoli, P., & Papadopoulou, M. (2012). *Graphic organizers as a reading strategy: Research findings and issues.* Creative Education, 3, 348–356.

Singleton, S. M., & Filce, H. G. (2015). *Reading comprehension for older readers.* Intervention in School and Clinic, 41, 131–137.

About the Authors

IAN BYRD

Ian taught gifted students in California where he grew up as a gifted kid himself. On his journey to become a teacher, he earned a degree in Computer Science, briefly played bass in an almost successful rock band, and married a fashion designer. Ian now lives in Portland, Oregon where he writes about gifted education at Byrdseed.com and develops videos for students at Byrdseed.TV.

LISA VAN GEMERT

Lisa grew up as a real, live gifted kid in California, where she devoured Nancy Drew mysteries and played soccer. She got a couple of degrees that let her teach elementary and high school, and then become an assistant principal. She was the Youth & Education Ambassador for Mensa, the expert consultant to some television shows about gifted kids, and she writes books about giftedness, including the award-winning *Perfectionism: A Practical Guide to Managing Never Good Enough*. She married an Australian software developer, and they have three sons. She writes about gifted ed at GiftedGuru.com.

NOTES

NOTES

NOTES

NOTES

NOTES

NOTES

Made in the USA
Monee, IL
10 November 2020